About the author

I have given many talks to libraries, clubs, two cruise ships and the Planetarium, and have sailed our beautiful west coast for forty years, Turkey, Greece, the Caribbean, across the USA, the Bahamas, Alaska and Southeast Asia. I am a retired civil engineer and business director in thirty-five countries. I owned nine sailboats, one of which my wife and I built from scratch in a remarkable three years in our garden and then sailed to the South Seas and Alaska.

Occasionally, it is good to sit back and dream of faraway places!

TRAVEL WITH ME

Do it now!

Patrick Hill

TRAVEL WITH ME

Vanguard Press

VANGUARD PAPERBACK

© Copyright 2021
Patrick Hill

A CIP catalogue record for this title is
available from the British Library.

ISBN 978 1 784659 36 3

*Vanguard Press is an imprint of
Pegasus Elliot MacKenzie Publishers Ltd.*
www.pegasuspublishers.com

First Published in 2021

**Vanguard Press
Sheraton House Castle Park
Cambridge England**

Printed & Bound in Great Britain

Dedication

To those who are seeking travel, adventures, exploring and new cultures.

Perhaps you are Cathy, and I think you will enjoy this memoir of mine, I wrote it and have enjoyed it.

So best wishes from

Patrick Hill

2023

Acknowledgements

My Thanks

My thanks go to my wife, Heather, with her warm and unstinting support for all our plans since we first met; to our children, Jeremy and Erica, who are equally positive and supportive of my actions; and, of course, to our grandchildren, Riley, Ellen, and Kira.

Thanks also go to Heather for the use of her diary in which she has diligently described every day since 1958. Her entries have bought to the surface so many events that would have remained submerged in the fog of time.

My thanks also go to Rose Dudley and Dr John Gould for reading the book and to friends Luigi Guzy and Don Monroe for their encouragement.

TRAVEL WITH ME

"As an eagle takes flight
And is borne above the clouds
So must I spread my wings
And embrace the power of the wind."

Richard Elliott, Whistler Mtn., bc

Previous Books

So Where Do You Go at Night?
(Also titled: *Home on the Waves*)
A 15,000-mile, 14-month family
sailing adventure to exotic atolls,
South Seas islands and Glacier
Bay, Alaska
(Chapters, Barnes and Noble, Amazon)

GBS 5 Years Later
Co-author of my experience with
the rare Guillain-Barre Syndrome,
which paralyzed me for a month
(Trafford)

Explore the Alaskan Coast
A rare sailing trip exploring glaciers
from Prince William Sound to Glacier
Bay including Yakutat Bay and the
uninhabited Icy and Lituya Bays
(Amazon & self-published)

French Silk on Water
Sailing across
The Great Lakes, through the
Erie Canal, New York, and Miami
to the Bahamas
(Amazon & self-published)

A New Life in Canada
(Ungram Spark)

Books also available from
www.patrickhillcruising.com
hphill@telus.net

Contents

Foreword

This book is a memoir of my life and the adventures I have experienced and thoroughly enjoyed in different environments with Heather, my wife. Many of these adventures resulted from opportunities that suddenly arose and we took immediate advantage of. It is part of my philosophy of "do it soon — do it now," a belief that has grown over time, perhaps from schooldays, to take an opportunity to do something new. When you read this, I hope you identify chances that will enliven your time here.

After evacuation and wartime in London, I left school and was drafted into the army in Germany. When I was a free man again, I became an engineer. I met Heather at a tennis club dance, travelled with her on and off for four years before bursting out one night with a proposal to marry and live together. With her acceptance, we married and emigrated to Canada. Three years later our son Jeremy was born, and with work slowing down, we moved yet again to northern Australia. After working there and exploring the Outback, we returned to the UK for more study. A year later we resettled in beautiful Vancouver, learning to ski and sail. Our daughter Erica was born. After exploring the coastline, we built a boat and sailed to the exotic South Seas and then back to the Alaska coast. More trips and travels followed whenever we found time or the occasion arose. We work on the principle that you should take every opportunity to experience at least some of the many adventures available.

This story is not about World War II, but because it provides a perspective about my past life, I have included a list of the key events in the Appendix.

As a much-travelled civil engineer, my story often leads the reader from one prospect to the next with an intermix of work experiences, social and family life. Although it does not refer back more than three or four generations, it does explain my background and my earlier life, particularly in London, because over time there has been a remarkable change in our thinking and the way we live. I would like my children, grandchildren, and any who follow to understand and appreciate our family background and perhaps add to our history.

Dream, enjoy life, and visualize a different experience for a while.

Patrick Hill, West Vancouver
www.patrickhillcruising.com

With Best Wishes to Cathy Forand

When thinking about things to do — just do it now!

Patrick Hill

2023

CHAPTER 1

Early Life in London
1932–1939

I guess my arrival in the world was as something of a tail-end Charlie, wartime slang for the rear gunner in a Lancaster bomber. I wonder what my elder brothers, Michael, Raymond, and Tony aged 12, 10, and 8 thought about my arrival after an eight-year gap, let alone my parents.

I was born at 18a Cedars Road, Clapham, London where no doubt I was held up by a midwife and likely given a slap or two to start my breathing as Patrick Norman Milford Hill on March 8, 1932. My parents were William Hill III, journalist and author, and Nora Josephine Hewitt, spinster, who lived at 26 Deanville Court, Clapham.

My mum retained her single status because she worked for a major newspaper which had a policy of not hiring married women. I did not know my brothers and I were illegitimate until I received a letter from Michael when I was 26. I was later to learn there was another reason why my mum remained unmarried.

My family has a connection going back on my father's side to James Hill, a baker born in 1793 and on my mum's side to the Godolphin family (Cornwall) in 1681. William Hill I was born in 1804. My grandfather, William Hill II, was born in 1852 and died in 1932 at the age of 80, shortly after I was born. I wonder if he held me after my birth. My father, William Hill III, was born in 1886. My grandfather was a journalist of some note. His obituary noted:

He came from Tynemouth in northern England and played a notable part in newspaper enterprises... bringing to Fleet Street the grit, independence, and persistence characteristic of the Northerner.

He cherished the idea of a Liberal London newspaper, later established the *Tribune* and became managing editor.

He enjoyed the friendship of Lord Morley, Lord Milner, and Lord Oxford.

He was director of the City of London School for Journalism where students applied for the 400 GBP Stevens Scholarship — a significant sum in 1902, which could buy a house. My grant in 1952 for engineering studies was a mere two GBP per week, barely enough to take a girl out.

In 1898 he visited Palestine as a journalist and from what can be determined from his diary, met the Sultan and the German Kaiser while on tour. His conclusions on the visit: "The Holy Land is one of the most dreary lands that man could enter" and "There are at least several ways for a tourist to die in Jerusalem, at any rate, this week: 1. Sun, 2. Pavements, 3. Smells, 4. Dust, and 5. Baksheesh."

He was awarded the Silver Cross of the Order of the Redeemer by His Majesty the King of the Hellenes in recognition of work he had carried out on behalf of Greece. He certainly led an active life in the newspaper world as I was to find my mum and father also did.

Following the death of my grandfather, our family moved to his house at 15 Old Park Avenue, Clapham, south London until 1942. It was one of two large attached redbrick houses of four stories where I lived for ten years. Off the hall, the front room and the back room, with its verandah to the garden, was occupied by father's parents and sister, Jenny. At the rear of the house a large, dark and dreary kitchen, scullery and pantry provided me with a place to explore. In the summer, food was cooled by evaporation from a damp cloth. A back door led out into the garden, and an outside toilet, where the water tank was located high above the toilet and operated by a chain. In the winter it was always chilly and sometimes I was tempted to use an indoor flowerpot. Stairs led down to the cellar where coal was delivered. Exploring here was a bit frightening, as it was a really dim area, always cold and musty.

The main stairs with dark wood bannisters led up one floor to a small kitchen then continued up a short flight leading onto a landing with our parents' bedroom, our living room, toilet and bathroom. Two more floors above led to more bedrooms. Down the middle of the house, the stairwell was perhaps some 30 to 40 feet deep. Often for a challenge, my brothers would climb up the stairs on the outside of the bannisters. Sometimes I tried this, but once I got about eight feet up it was either too scary or Aunt Jenny would appear, demanding that I come down. The upper part of the house was occupied by our family.

Initially, lighting was by gas mantles but later all lighting was converted to electric. In those early days, the streetlights were lit by gas. In the evenings, a man would cycle to each light and with a long pole, reach up and turn on the light.

In the morning, bottled milk was delivered to the house by the milkman from his red horse-drawn cart. He whistled to the horse to keep up with him. The streets had no parked cars to hinder him in those days. If you got the bottle first, you might be lucky enough to get the rich cream at the top. Sometimes the rag and bone man would come around with his horse and cart ringing a bell and calling out for your junk. A man on a bicycle might also call, asking if we needed our knives sharpened. Droppings from horses would be collected for manure and enterprising lads collected it and sold it. Heather told me her grandmother always said, "Quick, get it while it's hot!" I was not given a reason for the rush except perhaps to get it before anyone else.

Our house had no phone, only a radio crystal set in an ornate three-legged cabinet. We had to manipulate the crystals to hear a program or get the latest news. Watching my father or brothers adjusting various pieces of the set while listening with earphones, I was surprised to suddenly hear a weak voice speaking through the background crackling. The crystal sets worked with no external power. Raymond told me our father was very clever at making radios, using speakers instead of earphones, which hung on the side of the wood cabinet.

Using W. Wimbledon Hill as a *nom de plume*, my father

followed in the journalistic footsteps of our grandfather. He obtained a BA (economics, law) from Trinity College, Cambridge where he rowed in the "Bump" races at the age of 20. His oar was always hung on a wall in the sitting room.

Armed with a grant by Lord Northcliffe at the City of London School he travelled widely as a journalist. He crossed the Andes in 1910 on a mule, when the Transandine Rail Tunnel, peaking at 10,000ft, from Buenos Aires to Valparaiso, was under construction; travelled through the Panama Canal, interviewing the US Army colonel in charge; and visited the USA (twice), Canada, Europe, Japan, and India studying trade and social conditions. He then worked at *The Times* (being reorganized by Lord Northcliffe), the *Daily Mail, Sunday Express, Daily Mail,* and on the *Evening Standard*. He published the *Official Centenary Souvenir History of the Oxford and Cambridge Boat Race* (1829–1929). He was even presented with a silver trophy by the Honorable Theodore Roosevelt for his work in journalism. He seemed to have his own "do it now" motto.

I'm disappointed I did not hear about his adventures and cannot recall they were ever mentioned. Nothing was passed on that would have increased our perspective on life.

My mum worked as a secretary to key staff, including authors Leonard Mosley, the paper's film critic, and Bernard Wickstead, in the editorial department of the *Daily Express*. Many times, when I was around 12, I took the train to London, then bus up to Fleet Street, entered the very modern *Daily Express* building and asked for her at reception. The building was close to Ludgate Circus, which was left in ruins after a German V2 rocket landed there.

While I waited for her, there was a continual call of "Boy!" and some young lad would be dispatched to deliver a message or package somewhere in the building. In a while, my mum swept down the stairs into the lobby, gave me a warm hug, and we went off somewhere to have a meal or, for a special treat, to a restricted review evening of a new film. We sat in the plush seats of a nearly empty Curzon Theatre on Curzon Street or some other smart cinema and enjoyed a new film such as *Tunisian Victory*, or we went to a theatre and saw Peter Ustinov in *The Love of Four Colonels*.

In those days, some film theatres had an organist who played at the beginning or in the interval. During the interval, you could go down to the front where a girl with a tray sold chocolates, cigarettes or ice cream. The main film was usually accompanied by a short Movietone film giving all the latest news. During the war, we always wanted to know if the British troops were advancing because it raised our spirits. When going to a play, my mum, while buying our tickets, would rent a small numbered stool to place in the line outside the theatre to hold our place in the queue. This allowed us to go off for a snack without waiting around. So civilized! After our evening out, we got a bus back to Victoria railway station, a train back to Banstead, and walked up to our home. On the way back, we discussed the film or what I had done during the day. Her interest was so strong and although it was possibly a big effort for her after a long day at the office, I'm sure she enjoyed it as much as I did.

My mum always had a ready feeling for others, especially looking after her mum and taking her to a film once a week. She was exceedingly generous, tolerant, forgiving and most industrious, giving her time and energy to all of us and even more distant family members. She rarely complained although I sometimes heard her arguing with my father. With her radiant smile, she was such a warm and friendly person. I would often meet her at the local railway station at 6 or 7 p.m. after her hour's journey from London, to carry her parcels. I doubt I ever fully appreciated the effort she made on my behalf, which would have been cooking a meal for us that night as well as shopping during the day, if I had not been asked to do it. In 1950 she bought an Austin 7, a marvellous little car with coloured indicator arms that flicked out to advise we were going left or right. We both learnt to drive it. She was expected to retire at the age of 60 but did not do so until she was 68, telling her bosses she had forgotten how old she was. My father and mum worked all their lives.

Up to the start of World War II (1939–1945), life with my three brothers was a kaleidoscope of activities such as fighting, playing noisy games, inventing new games and leaping down the stairs, such that my mum would occasionally use a cane to maintain some level of control. My brothers would often retreat to my bedroom to compare the weals she had inflicted upon them. During the day we were looked after by an Irish maid, Kitty, and sometimes two maids who ran the house and us.

My brothers attended Clapham College near the Clapham South tube station. It was run by a group of Brothers. One, Brother Dunstan, would be invited to our house from time to time. We had some glasses that showed a girl dressed on the outside and nude on the inside. My family delighted in giving him a glass of beer and watching his reaction as he drank and all was revealed. He noted in Michael's school report that if he spent less time looking at himself in the mirror during physics, his marks would improve.

I had no idea what my brothers did at school, whether they were smart or athletic, other than Raymond left when he was 14 and Michael when he was 16. But it was when my brothers returned home from school that the fun started. Certainly, every family has a fund of "stories" that are told again and again at family gatherings and to newcomers. One story recounted letting go of my pram on a hill with me in it or the Brother Dunstan story or playing pontoon with Kitty. The family stories were inevitably embellished on each occasion, much like any good fishing yarn.

Michael and Raymond were very different characters, the former being calmer and more serious, the latter wild and more reactive. They were always fighting or challenging each other. I did not like the shouted arguments, did not wish to take sides and would often retreat to my room. Their clashes would show up in the sword fights conducted in the larger of their upper bedrooms.

In his travels, our father had collected many souvenirs, some of which were genuine swords. Tony would be the timekeeper for rounds, and the maid and I would be the spectators. While Michael attempted to fight scientifically with cunning one-handed actions, Raymond's approach was that of a wild Viking with two-handed slashing motions. The clang of sword hitting sword and their shouting was sometimes frightening. Why the maid allowed these fights is a good question, but she did, and it is surprising that no one was seriously injured since the swords were for killing, not for ceremonies. One day, however, Michael, in the heat of one of their "mock" battles, got hurt enough to scare Raymond, who tore out of the room and flew down the stairs with Michael in pursuit. In his anger, Michael tore a spear off the wall, and hurled it down the stairwell at Raymond where it stuck into the wooden stair, narrowly missing his feet.

In less physical pursuits, card games, crown and anchor, liar dice, the deadly spoons game, and Monopoly occupied much of the time. At one time, I knew every rent and price of the properties. The favourite card game was blackjack or pontoon, usually played with matchsticks as money. At any excuse, we would have a game. Sometimes, however, the game would develop into one of striptease. Of course, the maid, Kitty, was invited to play while my brothers played their darndest to get her to forfeit. Unfortunately for them, Kitty would arrive adorned with trinkets and many fern additions to her hair. Considerable skill at the game was required if their anticipated desire was not to be thwarted. Sometimes when we had two maids, my brothers tried to improve their play. Raymond told me that when the second maid played, they once wrestled with her to obtain a stocking she had lost until she fled to the toilet.

My Aunt Jenny, a nice wee soul, lived in the downstairs back room after the death of her parents and would often accost my mum or father on their return from work to complain about the antics and noise going on upstairs or downstairs. Sliding on the bannisters or seeing how many of the last steps we could miss when jumping down was pretty noisy. Sometimes we climbed up the stairs on the outside of the bannisters where we could fall two or three floors if the bannisters broke. Jenny had some justification for her complaint as there was always shouting or a wild game going on.

One day, Tony was in the garden showing his friend his

stamp album when Michael, who had just acquired an airgun, shot from a window above. The pellet struck the book and damaged a stamp or two. Tony immediately demanded that he take a shot at Michael or else he would tell mum. It took a bit of digging to retrieve the pellet from Michael's arm. Sometime later, Tony got hold of the gun and while my mum was washing up at the sink, stuck it in her back demanding, "Hands up or I shoot!" She replied, "Don't be silly. I'm busy." So, he shot her. Talk about living dangerously. In those days, whalebone corsets were in style and this, fortunately, spread the blow into a rather large bruise, which was considerably smaller than the sum of the bruises she then inflicted upon him. *Did I say she was tolerant?*

Aunt Jenny always had a store of Cadbury's chocolate bars in the drawer beside her bed, and I soon learned that I had to chat her up for a while before she would offer me a piece. After she died, I realized I'd had more success with her than when I went to a local sweet shop during the war and told the man I wanted a bar of his under-the-counter chocolate after saying my father worked for the Admiralty. No luck there.

There was always something going on, and I recall Tony telling me that this particular Sunday afternoon he was going to launch his newly made model boat in the bath after he herded all the aunts and uncles into the bathroom. He gave me two pennies: one for me, if I threw the other into the bath just after the boat was launched. Well, amid the clapping at the launch, I threw the penny into the bath, creating an obligation such that the invited guests felt obliged to follow with a shower of coins. It was an early entrepreneurial lesson.

On Saturdays, Tony, Cousin Derek (the son of my mum's only sister, Tessa, who lived a few houses away in our road), and I often walked to Woolworth's close to the Balham railway station. For a penny we would buy a part-filled box of broken biscuits which we would consume while sitting on a brass bar inside the entrance of the store. Being the smallest, I never got a chance at the pieces covered with sugar coating. Two self-service cafes, Lyons and ABC, had cards and draughts available so we could play there while downing a cake or two. Tony and I were always playing draughts.

Our parents took us on regular annual holidays to Birchington and Margate in north Kent. Lynton, Lynmouth, and Woolacombe were their favourite holiday places.

We stayed in guesthouses, with our parents in one room and we brothers in another. On being shown our room there was a rush to get the best bed, and I usually ended up being close to the door. Many bed and breakfast places would not allow guests back into the house during the day, so some families had a tough day keeping their children amused and fed. Sometimes, a small shed (6x6ft) could be hired for the day for some privacy and to make a cuppa tea.

The beaches were wide swathes of firm sand that were great for cricket and ball games. While I wanted a game of cricket, my brothers might be using their code word *"deckchairs"* to alert one another — without my parents knowing — that a girl of interest was passing. One day though my mum said, "Look at those two nice deckchairs!" Raymond told me once that he and Michael had been in a beach cave and had just climbed up onto a rock shelf in the darkness when a girl came in and, to their delight, stripped off and changed into her bathing suit. They actually waited there until she came back to change.

Up to my teen years I seemed to suffer from a number of illnesses including chicken pox, measles and scarlet fever. The latter was highly contagious so my room had a sheet soaked in disinfectant hanging across the door at all times. When it was over, all soft toys had to be burned and others disinfected. Worse still were warts that invaded my hands, so that in kindergarten some children declined to hold hands when walking in pairs down the road, making me feel a bit of an outcast. Our family doctor, Dr. Smallwood, who was anything but small, always tested his weight on my bed before he sat on it to examine me. I even got a dose of infantile paralysis just before I started work. My efforts at getting back my physical condition were tough when I tried to run again.

In spite of the various illnesses I experienced, I guess I was lucky to have survived my pram days, because when my mum said to my brothers they had to take me on their walks, their favourite trick was to let go of the pram to see how fast it could go down a hill before they caught it. It was one of our more dramatic family stories.

William Hill II
Grandad

William Hill III
Father

Grandad on the left >>>

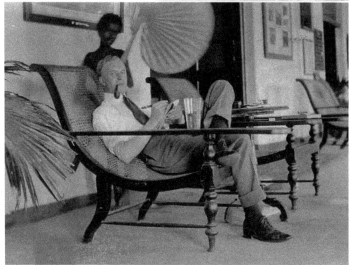

Father in some exotic place.
Note pipe and turn-ups

Mum in earlier times

Dad in Yokohama riding
in a jinrikishan

Mum near retirement

Gran - Note tea pot in hearth. She
always had a whiskey with her tea

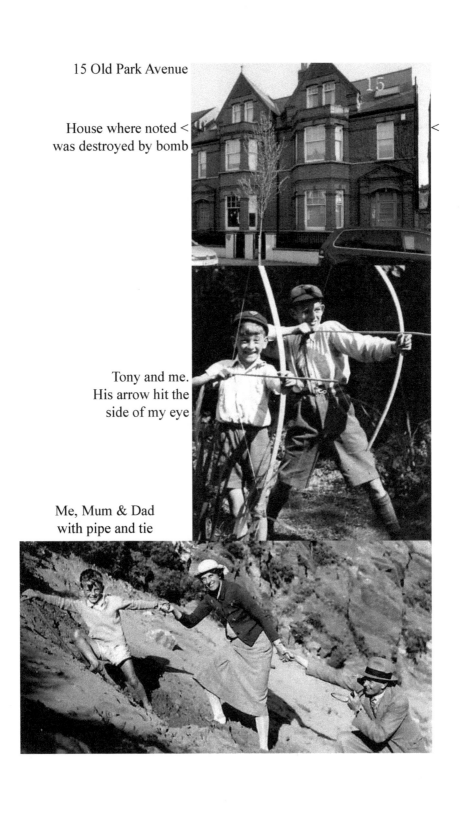

15 Old Park Avenue

House where noted <
was destroyed by bomb

Tony and me.
His arrow hit the
side of my eye

Me, Mum & Dad
with pipe and tie

City of London
Freemens School

Mum
Mike
Me
Derek
Audrey
Tony
at 25 Green Curve

Ray
Me
Tony waving
Mike
Tony is always lifted up when
brothers meet.

Deb, Me, Barry, Richard, Wendy, Mike, Anne,
Molly, Heather, Jane, Ray, Lallian, Michelle, Angela

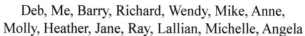

A Spitfire flying over   V1 doodle-bug.

A Spitfire wing-tipping a V1 doodle-bug.

Barrage against low flying aircraft.
Source of pictures above:
Imperial War Museum

My mum doing gas mask drill at her offic

Source of pictures below Wikipedia.
People finding their way to work amid bomb damage after a night raid

Me driving a Bren gun
carrier. Hit 55 mph.

Came 2nd in 440yds sports
competition, Dormund,
Germany during army service.

Roger, Heather, Me,
Chris, Helen.

Heather receiving Cup
and flowers at famous
Wimbledon Tennis Club,
by winning finals of
16-round London Parks
Tournament at age 17

After a night in a Paris police station.

Heather leaping over Le Touquet.

X-ing the Channel.

On the Eiffel Tower.

Hitchhiking is fun.

A just-met selfi

Exploring canals of Venice

The SS Caslon which
brought me to Canada.

My monster car having
the tire changed by friends
using a plank to raise car
while I watch.

American Soo locks can be
seen from the Windsor Hotel
where I lodged in Sault Ste.
Marie in background.

Mum's fun VG
Austin Ruby which
we both drove.

13th July, 1957

Michael, Mum, Raymond, Me, Heather, Jane, Helen, Chris

Me, Ray, Mum, Michael, Tony

Back in
Montreal.

Heading
for Calgary
Edmonton.

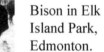

Bison in Elk
Island Park,
Edmonton.

Heather keeping warm.   Big horn ram on highway.

A wild landing at Cape May, east coast, USA

Use body weight or chains to climb Mt. Baker.

Viewing Grand Canyon on scary mules.

CHAPTER 2

Wartime Life
1939–1945

In the years I was growing up, our lives were influenced by the shadow of Hitler's ambitions leading to World War II. I sometimes heard my parents or visitors talking about Hitler and Prime Minister Chamberlain. Hitler's mega plans to control the territories of Europe, and perhaps the world, grew insidiously until he caused the start of World War II in 1939. I have given a simplified outline of key events in the Appendix as to why it started and how it was concluded because I think it interesting to have an understanding of this war.

1939

September 1: Germany attacked Poland from the west and Russia attacked from the east on September 17.

September 3: To meet their treaty obligations, Britain, Australia, New Zealand and France declared war against Germany — a second world war with Germany within 21 years.

By 1939 I was beginning to see signs of protective devices being installed such as pillboxes and tank traps, and increased military movements. These preparations were underway prior to the declaration of war, causing disruption to many families, including ours. Michael (19) went into service with Kodak on special photographic work. Raymond, who had left school when he was 14, had a job in a printing company which father had found for him, but he did not like that and left home. He joined the Home Guard, applied to get into the Palestine Police but was rejected, and finally joined the army when he was 17. During this time, he met Lillian, and they were married in June 1944. He went to Egypt the same year but was injured and rehabilitated in Switzerland. We didn't see him again until the war ended. When I started writing this memoir, he told me he had seen the British zeppelin R101 when it was on a flight to France, where it crashed in October 1930.

Because of the war, a million children were evacuated from London to less vulnerable parts of the country to avoid being bombed by the German air force. I was evacuated in 1939 to Ashtead in Surrey some 15 miles south of London. On the way there, the train stopped because of an air raid siren, one of the first we had heard. I was curious and wanted to see what was happening, but my mum quickly put all the cushions against the windows to protect us from flying glass should a bomb fall nearby. She was so smart. We heard nothing and proceeded to the home of Madame Boniface, with whom I was to stay.

Madame Boniface was a widow and ran a small primary school in her living room. I felt quite intimidated as I was shown to my bedroom, a small room over the garage with a sloping ceiling and a small round porthole window at each end. On leaving, my mum said, "Your father and I want you to stay here as Hitler might be bombing us, and we think you will be safer down here. Madame Boniface will look after you and we will come and visit you whenever we can. Tony will be here soon so you will have his company." Then, with a loving hug she was gone, leaving me lonely for quite a while.

Madame Boniface had hair on her chin. She wanted to bathe me, but I declined that. She had a son, Victor, who was in the army.

Her spotted dog, Chum, became my good companion. Each day I would attend a class composed of about seven or eight children of my age or younger. I spent two years there. Tony joined me later but stayed at another house. After school, I would ride my bike in the neighbourhood or end up at a nearby stream trying to dam it. It was perhaps my first thoughts about "do it now" as a civil engineer.

Madame Boniface always closed school on Wednesday afternoon, and we would drive into the nearby town of Epsom in her Morris 8 car to see a film. The trouble was that she had no idea how to back the car out of the garage. It became my job (at age 8) to provide directions. She could not always see or hear me standing at the back of the car and could get quite flustered. One time, she managed to jam the rear fender into the brick wall, so the car could not move forwards or backwards and a man had to be brought in to extract it; no film that week. I suggested a new way of doing this, which worked fine thereafter. I stood on the running board, reached through the window and steered the car while she worked the pedals. For a while, I also gave directions for her coming into the garage, but it later proved unwise to stand at the end of the garage doing this as once she rammed the end wall where I would normally stand. Luckily, I had enough sense 'to do it early' before I got hurt.

At the beginning of the war we experienced many changes to our daily lives. Gas masks were issued to everybody and it was necessary to carry them at all times. I found my face mask horrible, smelly and initially claustrophobic, which did not encourage its use. Most civilian masks were kept in 7 x 8 x 8-inch cardboard boxes with a shoulder strap. Car lights were covered over so that only a thin horizontal slit of light could be seen.

Some cars were set up with a gas balloon on the roof and these cars ran on methane gas because of the shortage of gasoline. Railway coach windows were blackened so that no light could be seen from the air. Destination signs were virtually eliminated so that a stranger, who might have been a spy, would have difficulty finding his way, and likely bring suspicion upon himself. Signs went up advising people not to talk to strangers and certainly not to discuss any topics to do with war, in case there were spies about. Poles were erected in fields to prevent the landing of enemy planes or gliders. Anyone who looked suspicious or had an accent was to be reported. Main entrances to buildings had sandbag protection walls built.

Rationing started in England in January 1940. Ration cards for food were issued and were marked up by shopkeepers when the weekly allowance of butter (2 oz.), bread (1 loaf), meat (12 oz.), bacon (4 oz.), eggs (2), and sugar (8 oz.) were purchased. All food and confectionary were rationed, but it was often thought people ate better than before the war. When I went shopping, I took the ration books and handed them over to be marked up when buying rationed food.

Later, when U-boats sank so many British supply ships, rationing became more stringent. Clothing was rationed too. To save materials, a man's suit must have no turn-ups, only three buttons and three pockets. Clothes were recycled or re-used or modified. Gasoline (petrol) was also rationed as were cigarettes. Owners often removed the rotor arm of a car's ignition system to prevent theft.

A black market developed whereby "extras" were obtained under the counter. Gasoline was frequently siphoned out of someone else's car because tanks were not locked. Rationing was finally discontinued in 1954, nine years after the end of the war, an indication of the state of England's economy.

Everyone was issued with identity cards. Iron fences were pulled down and melted down for steel production. I collected my father's used razor blades, but arrangements were set up with locals to collect old razor blades, paper, and any material that could be used in the war effort; later in my Boy Scout days, two or three of us would take a cart around to collect any of these materials from people's homes; sometimes we were offered cakes. Tape strips were put across windows to reduce the dangers of flying glass from bomb blasts. At night, blackout curtains covered all our windows. Air raid wardens went around at night, and there would be a heavy knock on the door if you had a light showing — you would be told in no uncertain terms, "Get those bloody lights out." At the time, it was thought that the Germans could see a cigarette glowing in the streets from the air.

Air raid shelters were built in public places and on people's properties. Our garden in Clapham was dug up and an Anderson shelter was installed. The shelter was made of corrugated galvanized steel plates on a concrete base half-buried in the ground and the rest covered with earth. It was about 7 by 8ft and had a small entrance with steps into it and a bench down both sides. When an air raid warning sounded with its undulating siren, we left the house, sometimes reluctantly, armed with blankets, drinks, snacks, and card games and waited there until the "all-clear" siren sounded.

Sometimes it was quite cold out there or, in the summer, a good place to chat with a friend. Later, we had a Morrison shelter inside the house. This had about the same area but was built with a steel plate supported in each corner by four steel posts sitting on a steel frame on the floor. Wire mesh around the outside was supposed to stop debris falling inside. We, of course, had the cellar which, when the coal and junk was cleaned out, was quite an effective shelter except that if the house collapsed on top of it, we might all be buried.

Life passed pleasantly along in these early days, with little sign of the actual war except for the many Canadian soldiers who were camped under the trees near the Ashtead railway station (I met one later when I worked in Montreal). This period was called the Phony War because there was no sign of the Germans or their planes. It continued to about April 1940 when the word "Blitzkrieg" was heard, Germany's new technique of speed and surprise movement which required the evacuation of British troops from Dunkirk. With the Germans trying to eliminate the British air force we experienced the Battle of Britain. Sometimes on a clear day, I could see high up in the blue sky a "dogfight" in progress. On occasions, a British fighter would pass low overhead waggling its wings, a sign of success.

Later, Hitler changed his attack to a massive bombing blitz of London lasting six months, in an attempt to bring the populace to its knees and surrender. But it had the opposite effect in further uniting the spirit of the people against Germany.

Afterwards, a "V for victory" hand sign began and could frequently be seen. At the same time the "dot, dot, dot, dash" Morse signal for "V" began on the radio. These signals were to encourage the population and occupied peoples that we were winning and to be hopeful.

I do not recall missing my parents, although they only came

to see Tony and me from time to time. It would have been a tough job for them to take a train from London to come and see us. We went for a walk, visited a tea shop, and then I was returned to Madame Boniface. Tony had got himself a job with the local hardware store delivering paraffin fuel in a pushcart. Sometimes I went with him on his rounds. On the return journey, I might ride in the cart, but this was potentially dangerous as on occasions he would deliberately let go of the handles on a downhill slope. It was then Tony told me that when my brothers were told to take me out in the pram for a walk, they used to let the pram go down the hill and, at the last possible moment, rush forward and catch it. Nice guys!

One time, we were in the woods above Ashtead station and Tony said, "I have some matches. Let's start some fires." This we did, but we usually put them out before they were out of control. The inevitable occurred, and we had to rush away from a scene of flames higher than ourselves. We returned as innocents, when Canadian soldiers from nearby had put the fire out. Tony only lasted some six months before getting fed up with his life away from home and rode on his bike all the way back to London to join our parents. For me, this was a tremendous step into the unknown, and I was lonely for a while after he had gone.

I spent much of my spare time reading, especially a book I found called *The Coral Sea* about a family living on a remote island. It probably initiated my interest in sailing. I would take Chum for walks, but he was a strong dog and could drag me through the ferns if he went after something. Once, he caused both of us to fall into the local river. We were both shivering and I was chastising him when a passing lady thought I was frightening him and wanted my name and address. Later that day, a policeman called on Madame Boniface. It was my first encounter with the law. On another occasion the police called when a lady thought I had deliberately smashed a bottle on the road and she reported it. All this in the middle of a major war.

A partial state of hunger used to exist, although I refused to eat tapioca desserts. It became a battle of wills between myself and

Madame Boniface as I was made to sit at the kitchen table in front of any unfinished food. Once, when searching around, I found a few pennies under the paper liner in a drawer and was able to buy five fresh bread rolls and gorge myself in the woods while reading my book.

Madame Boniface was fairly strict when she was running her little school. One day she put Jilly in detention at the bottom of the stairs when I was drying up after lunch. I started making her laugh by putting a bowl on my head and making funny faces. When Madame heard all this laughter and saw I was the cause, she took a solid round wood ruler, one inch in diameter, and smashed it down on the back of my hand, leaving me crying in pain as I rushed up to my room. From this school, I went to the City of London Freemen's School in Ashtead in 1941.

In mid-1942, the two terraced houses next door to us on Old Park Avenue were hit by a bomb. It was after this bombing, while my parents were looking for a safer place to live close to my school in Ashtead, that I left Madame Boniface and joined my parents in Clapham for the summer holidays. The area received its share of bombing and many times we retired to the chill of the outside Anderson shelter or our cellar when an air raid was on. Following the siren, I would hear the muffled thump of anti-aircraft guns, the engines of the bombers, and then the whine of falling bombs and the crump of their explosion. I often got a glimpse of searchlights sweeping across the sky looking for bombers. In the daytime, I could see silvery barrage balloons, a defence against low-flying planes. After a raid, Tony, our cousin Derek and I would search for shrapnel in the streets. We always kept an eye out for a small hole in the ground that would indicate the presence of a shell cap, a valued prize for trading with other kids.

The now derelict properties next door provided an excellent play area for the stone fights which we engaged in with Derek and others. I remember the time I peered round a fence only to receive a stone that Tony had been waiting to throw, full blast on my forehead. It was not as bad as the arrow he once shot into the side of my eye. I did get my own back once by dropping a bag of soot on him as he climbed out of a window below me. Perhaps these were lessons in survival while we roamed the adjacent bombed-out ruins pursuing the dangerous game of stone fighting until the helmet of a "bobby" appeared.

The buildings always smelled of damp plaster and decay. Our house was supported by angled supports against its exposed wall until it was repaired. The houses next door, were taken down and rebuilt after the war.

In 1942 my parents found a three-bedroom flat at 4 Eastgate, Banstead, further out of town and close to my school. My parents, Tony and I lived there till 1944. Michael sometimes came down from London alone or with his girlfriend for the weekend. Tony and I would have tremendous games of draughts and furious fights would develop when Derek came to stay. Tony had an amazing artistic talent of being able to draw lifelike dog fights of old planes, biplanes whizzing in and out of clouds, and some spiralling down in smoke. At that time fighter planes were often seen and later we saw many doodlebugs rocketing overhead. The war was still going full blast, blackouts were still required, and listening to the daily news was a must as the news was not always good.

A little restaurant, the Rendezvous, directly opposite our flat and where I often had lunch, was hit by a bomb. I helped clear up the mess for some days and the owners were thankful. At times, incendiary bomb drills would take place for our air raid wardens. A smoke bomb would be let off on the green behind our flat and a team of two would try to put it out, one crawling forward holding a hose above his head while the other person pumped water from a bucket using a stirrup pump — all very entertaining. At this time, Tony had joined the Air Training Corps, and when my father was going after him for some misdeed, he advised my father (with some innovation, I must say), "You cannot strike me. I'm wearing the king's uniform." This did not deter my father, who gave him a good wallop.

In June 1943, Tony (19) enlisted in the army as a dispatch rider delivering mail to Churchill's home, Chartwell, in Kent. A year later he embarked for France and Germany where he was wounded. My mum and I used to visit him in a nearby army hospital (Belmont) where all the injured military wore bright blue jackets and trousers, white shirts, and red ties. He left the army in June 1947 with a pension of some 2GBP (pounds) per week.

In 1944–45, towards the end of the war, when I was in Devon during the summer holidays, I would see and hear waves and waves of bombers overhead, Hallifaxes, Lancasters, Handley Pages, American Flying Fortresses, and Mosquitos on their way to bomb a target in Germany. The fortunes of war were being reversed. During my school years, the war continued with key events outlined in the Appendix.

In the final stages of the war, Hitler, in his desperate attempt to demoralize Londoners, sent over thousands of V1 rockets, known as doodlebugs or buzz bombs. We could hear the distinct roar of their motors, particularly at night, and then an abrupt stop. If we thought one had stopped right overhead, we were normally safe because it would glide on for a while before turning into a vertical dive and exploding. If it seemed to have stopped far off, then we might be in trouble.

They finally stopped coming in March 1945, but in my holidays, I must have seen over 50 in the sky and saw some dive into the ground followed by rising smoke and an explosion. Sometimes I saw a Spitfire chasing one.

On VE Day, or Victory in Europe Day, there was exhilaration and rare gaiety in the air as people relaxed and generally went mad. In London we pushed our way through the massive crush of people in Trafalgar Square, many having fun in the fountains, many hugging and dancing, while I hung onto my father's coat belt so I did not get lost in the press of people. We ended up in a hotel restaurant where my parents got up and danced. Street parties were held all over Britain, and any passing military person was often treated with considerable passion.

In 1945, after two years at Eastgate, we moved to 25 Green Curve about half a mile from Eastgate. My parents, Tony and I lived there. Michael, who had started a specialized photographic business in London, married Joan, an ex-petty officer in the Wrens and lived locally.

During the war, my father worked at the Admiralty, the government offices responsible for naval affairs. I later learned that his job had been to debrief the crews of those saved from ships sunk by German U-boats and planes. Our losses in those days had been terribly serious, to the point of almost causing us to lose the war. He often had an air of distraction about him, possibly because of the unpleasant news he was recording. He could not discuss this with my mum because the news was withheld from the public.

Little wonder he did not give me the attention I would have liked. In May 1946 he had a stroke. Mum and I visited him in hospital and I recall being much embarrassed when she turned to me and said he had asked her to help him with the pee pot. He did not fully recover and died later that year, saddening news to all of us, especially to mum, along with my brothers, who had to look after me and the finances. I do not recall a funeral service. It was a shame that I did not have a stronger relationship with my father. He had such a wide experience of the world and business life, which would have been wonderful to have glimpsed and might have encouraged a closer relationship.

CHAPTER 3

School Days
1941–1948

The school I went to in 1941 was one of two co-educational boarding schools in England. I was one of many lowly dayboys. According to its mandate, it originally opened for orphans of the City of London.

The 300-acre grounds with a cricket green, rugby fields and tennis courts were magnificent. The dormitories, dining hall, and staff rooms were in a large Georgian building, originally the Manor House of Ashtead. Nearby was a 12th-century church and graveyard nestled among sweeping, ancient cedars. The original stables formed a quadrangle surrounded by classrooms and an assembly area. The school was in session five and a half days a week with Wednesday afternoon for sports or, worse, for detention.

This was a happy time for me probably because for the first time I was meeting so many boys, learning new ideas, making friends and getting invited to homes. Although not particularly athletic, I enjoyed sports, except rugby and cross-country running. Throughout my school years, I played on a soccer team outside school with my best friend, Peter Giffen. When we first met at the school, he used to link arms with me as we walked together, something of a surprise to me.

Banstead was relatively near to the school in Ashtead Park. I used to take two buses or cycle the six miles to school. I learned quickly that drafting behind buses was a helpful if dangerous way to make the trip, as sometimes my front tyre would make a whirring noise rubbing on the back of the bus. The conductor frequently waved me away. At other times, several of us would have tremendous races on the way home. In winter, I was so cold on arrival at school, I would be allowed into the classroom before assembly to thaw out on the hot radiators, feeling the excruciating pain of recirculation.

At this time, it seemed winters were always cold, although the Little Ice Age (1250–1870) was allegedly coming to an end. At home, we had a coal fire in the main living room where we lived and ate our meals, sitting close to the fire, often with our feet in the hearth. The itching of chilblains caused by skin being exposed to too much cold became painful if too close to a source of heat. Curtains were doubled for insulation at the windows, and a cloth "sausage" was placed across the bottom of the door to keep the draft out. We always shut the door when going in or out, to keep the heat in. A paraffin stove was kept burning in the hallway to have some heat elsewhere in the house. On super cold days, this stove might be put up in the loft, the unused space under the sloping roof, to prevent the cold-water tank from freezing, and an electric fire, although expensive, might provide an extra source of heat.

In the morning, I rushed with my clothes from the warmth of my bed to the warmth of the nearby bathroom heated by the hot-water tank. The next source of heat was the kitchen, for breakfast, before leaving for work or school. At the end of the evening, the living room fire was carefully "banked" so it maintained heat as long as possible and might still be going in the morning. To help get the fire going, we held a sheet of the daily paper across the chimney opening to create a draft through the bottom of the fire. Sometimes, though, it would catch light and disappear up the chimney, and if we thought it was getting the chimney on fire, we had to throw salt on the fire. I held my pajamas in front of the fire to be warmed and after seeing them steam, I changed quickly and ran to my bed. Here might be another source of heat provided by mum — a hot-water bottle, often an old stone ginger beer bottle filled with boiling water and swathed in a woollen sock so my feet would not be scalded. In later years, when I was studying for four years in my small bedroom, I had an electric fire by my feet and a blanket over my back in winter.

My academic progress, or rather lack of it, must have made my parents despair. My report, featuring comments such as "31st out of 32 in the class this year… has done well," would surely not have been encouraging. I was once told I would not have a problem with arithmetic, but my favourite subject was geography. We were taught Latin but it seemed to have no earthly value except to cause mental anguish. A student friend and I halved our mutual problem with me covering the verbs and he the sentence construction, but this did not help when examination time arrived.

Progress, however, must sometimes reflect the teacher's ability and the relationship with a student to instil the appropriate motivation. Being struck on the back of my head by my French teacher's clenched fist and called a dumbbell led to fear on my part when he entered the classroom. He once knocked me right across my seat into the adjacent aisle. Of course, if one had performed well on the cricket or rugby school teams, which he coached, you were his favourite. I was not in that category. My great revenge, however, was to bowl him out in cricket practice one day when he took the bat from a student to demonstrate to our group how to deal with an off-break. When he commanded me to bowl to him, I felt this was my big chance to respond to all the indignities I had suffered. I carefully polished the cricket ball on my trousers for better smoothness, aligned my fingers at the best place on the seam to get maximum spin, took four or five paces, and let it go. I watched it fly through the air with a slight swerve knowing it looked good and as he stepped forward in his demonstration stroke, saw it hit the ground in front of his bat, kick sideways, slip between the bat and his leg and strike the wicket. I watched the bails fly off with great elation. He was out. As he looked at me, I asked, "Shall I bowl another one, sir?" with a slight emphasis on the sir.

Class behaviour normally ranged from absolute silence to absolute pandemonium, depending on the teacher. In reflection, I feel sorry for some teachers who would keep talking although they could hardly be heard over the noise, and who seemed to have abrogated their responsibility for control. We used various projectiles to idle away those 40-minute periods. We filled ink bombs from our open ink wells and put them on the ends of rulers to project them across the classroom. Our pen nibs were a more technical projectile. We broke off the tip, leaving two sharp spikes. Then we bashed the other end under a desk lid until it split sufficiently to slide a paper fin into. Then we projected it using a ruler.

Some teachers reacted violently at times, and I once saw a teacher holding a student by the scruff of the neck while he kicked him. On another occasion, a small boy was swung above a teacher's head. We often experienced formal caning by teachers, including myself, but more fearful was the treatment given by senior prefects. They could be violent and quite innovative in their treatment, should you dare to cross them. Of course, as we grew older our level of cheekiness increased to a maximum we felt could be tolerated without physical or punitive reaction. Our headmaster was a stiff, upright man we nicknamed Plank. During our physics lesson, we used to count the number of "ers" a teacher said. In a class once, we all rushed to the window to watch a parachutist drifting down, probably a disabled fighter, to land nearby.

We did not have many fights at our school, and I avoided most by befriending one of the stronger rugby players who was not an "in" boy. Perhaps it was because of the girls, although they were outnumbered by about 10 to 1. Close proximity in classes could be quite diverting. Without a fixed code of dress in most schools today, I wonder how boys can ever concentrate on their work. Rumours were always flying around that so-and-so had his hand inside her shirt, or that the matron had found a boy and the head girl in a linen cupboard. On being "allowed" to walk one day with some senior boys behind a group of girls, a whole new perspective opened up when one of the boys said, "Yes, but what's between their legs?"

Of course, we couldn't see any risqué film rated R unless we were 16 or accompanied by an adult, further restricting our knowledge of the opposite sex. So, when *The Outlaw* was showing with Jane Russell, complete with her extensive cleavage on display, it occasioned a new level of interest. Our Wednesday afternoons off were spent trying to get an adult to take us to the cinema's restricted films. At school lunch, girls sat at separate tables and each table was headed by a prefect to keep control. Some of the meals were so adhesive we could roll them along the tabletop. Semolina and tapioca desserts were particularly good rollers. When not at school, I cycled up to Banstead Village and bought lunch at a self-service style British Restaurant, a name chosen by Churchill. Often, when I came home from school, I made a jam sandwich and read my comics, *Hotspur*, *Champion* and others, swapped with friends, until my parents came home.

During breaks, we played soccer games with a tennis ball with considerable intensity to divert our attention from a lower to a higher plane. Another fine game was "kim ball" where one boy started off running, throwing a ball from hand to hand and chasing his victim. When he hit his victim with the ball the two then chased others, but could not run with the ball, only throw it to each other. When a third boy was hit, he joined the chasers until they were all chasing the last boy. Those being chased could defend themselves by punching the ball away with their fists or ducking at the last minute. We would return to class sweaty and covered in cinder dust from the playground.

Real speedway motorcycle racing was a sport some of us liked, and we developed our own speedway track using part of the school's gravel driveway. Groups of four would tear down the driveway at great speed and try to make a tight turn using a Norman Parker "foot forward" or an Oliver Hart "foot trailing" technique we had seen at speedway tracks. Then we'd cycle back to the starting point and around to do another circuit. Many a shiny new bicycle was severely damaged by these turns and the crashes that occurred, not to mention the scars accumulated by the riders. This pastime was finally called to a halt when the staff started noticing that their cars tilted over when driving past this point and so all participants spent our free Wednesday afternoon re-levelling the driveway. One unfortunate lad named Spy was being chased by a gang on bikes when one boy called to a friend further down the driveway, "Stop him," which he did by just touching his handlebar — the crash was horrendous, and his parents demanded an investigation.

I say there were few fights, but to get to our private school we had to pass a public school, and those students often lay in wait for us and stone fights or snowball fights developed as we tried to pass. Sometimes, a stone in a snowball did not encourage anyone to catch them.

In early 1947, a spate of infantile paralysis or polio occurred. This terrible and infectious illness could paralyze your nervous system to a point where an "iron lung" might be required to assist breathing. People could die from it. I seemed to have a mild dose of this and dreaded the possibility of it getting worse. I was in bed for three weeks being nursed by Joan, Michael's wife. During that time, I could not bend my head forward and was very much incapacitated. When I finally got to my feet again, I despaired for some weeks because trying to run was like slow-motion walking through water. I had a lot of catching up to do when I returned to school, all part of the catch-up now belief.

At the end of the school year, prizes were handed out, mainly in the form of bound and gilded books, to the top students and athletes. I didn't see myself ever getting one. The winning house, be it Gresham (mine), Hale, or Whittington would be acknowledged. A few prayers were said and then we sang *Jerusalem*, that marvellous hymn, with great gusto and were released for the wonderful seven weeks of summer holidays.

CHAPTER 4

Post-School Days
1948–1950

I took my school leaving certificate when I was sixteen in mid-1948 but, alas, obtained only four out of the six subjects required. While depressing for me, my mum encouraged me to obtain the certificate. Four of us, including one girl, were given an extra term of special coaching by an encouraging teacher. She began to make sense of history, literature, and other subjects, providing me with sufficient motivation to pass the two subjects I'd failed and so I got the certificate. As a present, my mum decided we would go on a holiday to Switzerland with my elder cousin, Derek. In reflection, I admire her for organizing such a holiday following the drudgery and stress of the war, while we were still on rationing, and given that her husband had only passed away two years earlier. It showed a determined spirit to get on with life.

We were excited as we trained down to Dover to board a ferry to cross the Channel, a natural defence which helped save England from a German invasion. At sixteen I loved the freedom this trip provided, although it looked like a rough crossing ahead, as there were buckets close to the gangway and some people were already being sick before the ferry even left the harbour. At sea, there was revolting bedlam in the saloon from people throwing up and, with the heavy rolling motion, one rather large lady who had fallen over, slid backwards and forwards in the smelly sick mess on the floor; nobody could help her. It was a relief to discharge onto land again in Calais.

The train to Basel was packed, and our carriage compartment was full, shoulder to shoulder, with eight people. After a few sandwiches as we roared through the night, conversation slowed, heads started nodding, drooping and swaying with the motion of the carriage. As the head of a young French girl next to me slowly came to rest on my shoulder, I found her breath was quite different from anything I had known. I was later to realize it was garlic. I also saw her dress had fallen forward, partially revealing the curve of her breasts in the dim light. With this exciting view, my imagination ran wild with the thought of actually placing my hand over one of them. Unfortunately, or fortunately, I lost my nerve in case it was not met with the same enthusiasm but with a loud scream. This delightful view certainly helped the journey pass more quickly.

At the Basel station, while waiting for the train to Lucerne, we were amazed to see white butter, jam, rolls, various meats, and many other goodies in unlimited quantities in the restaurant. As rationing was continuing in Britain, I was pleased to over-indulge in these luxuries. At the Hotel Johannaterhoff in Lucerne, the huge duvet on my bed was a surprise — something I had never seen before — as was the tremendous amount of food served. It must have been nice to be in a neutral country during the war.

After a funicular trip up Mt. Pilatus, I enjoyed the panoramic view of the mountains and sliding in the snow. I would have liked to stay longer, particularly because during the trip I had started a conversation with the girl having an intriguing cleavage. My mum invited her to join us that evening, so I was piqued to find I was to be left in the hotel and not taken to a night club. "Not old enough." Oh, yes?

My mum organized other trips for Derek and me, up the vertical lift on Mt. Rigi, a trip on the lake, Swiss flag-throwing demonstrations and hikes. The newness, cleanliness, and richness of what we saw in this neutral country must surely be a prime argument for avoiding wars.

I had read Edward Whymper's book, *Scrambles Amongst the Alps*, many times so I was delighted to see the mountains in Switzerland. When I had the opportunity to see more mountains, I could not wait to go — a "do it now" chance to the Outward-Bound School, Eskdale in the Lake District, run by Eric Shipton, a distinguished Everest climber. Michael, who had been providing colour consulting work for an Antarctic expedition, was invited to the school, but he suggested I go instead. My overnight train arrived at 6 a.m. in this remote station where a single man was waiting. I threw my rucksack out of the carriage window and followed it because the door would not open. We drove in his little open Austin through the lush hills and marvellous craggy dales to the school grounds where I stayed at his house. I had never driven in an open convertible car, so I was thrilled with the air flowing past, along with the wildness of the country.

I was allowed to join activities as I wished. I went cycling among the local hills on my own, did an all-day 20-mile hike with the group, which was an enjoyable challenge crossing moors and hills, and tried rock climbing. On discovering the school's abseiling practice rock with nobody around, I picked up the rope, and from previous reading of many climbing books, looped the line under one leg, then back over my shoulder and, with some hesitation, gingerly lowered myself backwards over the drop with my feet against the cliff face, down the 30–40-foot cliff. Once on the way, there was no going back.

When Eric took me rock climbing, I could not understand how he could stand so easily on a sloping rock face. I needed a lot more practice. When I went to say goodbye to his wife, I found her unfazed, breastfeeding her baby. I looked forward to my next "do it now" chance to be amongst steep hills and mountains.

When my parents found time for the three of us to go on a week's holiday, it would be to Lynton, Lynmouth, or the huge beaches at Woolacombe in Devon and in Margate, Kent. These were usually walking holidays along the cliff tops or beside a river. Generally, however, I looked after myself in the summer holidays as my parents were at work and my brothers elsewhere. In the time on my own, I delivered newspapers to local houses, attended scouting evenings or went cycling, played tennis or soccer with Peter Giffen and friends. I did the shopping, got my own meals and read. Sometimes my mum would bring back a tennis racket from her office where it had been left by some tennis star, which was good until the gut strings busted. My mum, who could play the piano, tried to teach me, encouraging me to practice, and I actually played the first part of the *Moonlight Sonata* and some other Beethoven pieces.

Our house was full of history books and I found myself continually searching through them for something that interested me. The ones I read most were about Sir Francis Drake, with their rich gold-embossed covers and the set of Arthur Mee's *The Children's Encyclopedias*. I found exciting stories of Drake overcoming Spanish Armada ships that were coming to land troops in England in 1588. Beating the Armada fleet with the use of bigger guns along with sending burning ships among the Spanish ships were tactics that really interested me.

Perhaps I was looking for a hero. In 1580, he returned from his famous three-year circumnavigation of the world, having got as far north as California if not Alaska. His continual and successful raids on Spanish ships and ports thrilled me as I read these stories for the first time.

Our Green Curve house, where we had moved from Eastgate, was a fairly typical detached English three-bedroom house located halfway up a hill. The end of the large garden backed onto remnants of the perimeter defence line of the greater area of London. This consisted of a huge continuous trench about 15 feet deep and 20 feet wide. Its purpose was to stop German tanks or other vehicles getting past. At regular intervals were concrete pillboxes aligned to fire upon the enemy. Concrete blocks were installed to stop tanks and vehicles crossing flat areas. This line of defence near us was set among large elm trees and provided a wonderful area for playing. My favourite pastime was building rope bridges across the trench and crossing in a somewhat perilous fashion. I used to spend a lot of time practising throwing an old, World War I bayonet and a curved Nepalese *kukri* knife into an old elm tree; sometimes, to my surprise, the *kukri* would hit the tree trunk on the curve of the blade and flash back towards me at great speed.

We played cricket on our large lawn and I was especially thrilled when my father came home and bowled to me, with an actual test match ball he had obtained from his office instead of the cork ball that was only available during the war. I frequently mowed this large lawn. In the winters, especially in 1947, we had so much snow I made a sledge with metal runners and joined others on a steep hill behind us. It was scary as I got up to full speed.

The weekends at any time over the years were a joy when family members, often with their girlfriends, joined my parents for an entertaining day or two of soccer or card games. Our favourite radio programs on a Sunday night, when they had all left, were the *Appointment with Fear* play or the Tommy Handley ITMA and the Frankie Howerd comedy shows, quite a change from listening to all the war news over the years.

The weekends were always interesting as Michael or Derek or both would come down from London on Sunday. Tony had his girlfriend, Audrey. When she came to meet mum, she ran down the front path, leaped through the front door and landed on the carpet, which slipped, dropping her smack on the floor. She just got up and laughed as we all did. After the war, Raymond, who was married in 1944, and had returned from convalescing in Switzerland, would come with his wife, Lillian. Once when Michael was making a lot of cheeky comments, she just kept loading jam onto a bread slice and then, with no warning, slapped him across the cheek with it. There were no more comments after that. If the boys came with a girlfriend, my mum would give each some tea and leave them in a room to themselves. She would generally end up in the kitchen ironing or cooking a roast. Before the roast dinner, we would amble up to the pub at Burgh Heath for drinks. Being underage, I sat outside with my fizzy drink. In the afternoon I might persuade them to play cricket or soccer or even have a try on the rope bridge. Sometimes we would walk together and play soccer on the downs.

Later there would be high tea followed by games of Monopoly, crown and anchor, whist, liar dice, or a wilder game called spoons. We played pontoon or blackjack the most, and on one occasion a strip game developed, and Tony's well-developed friend (and later wife), Audrey, stripped off her top in a very sporting fashion, which I found quite educational. Mum, who took everything in her stride, merely poured some more tea. Once she returned home to find Tony and Audrey in her bed, the only double bed in the house, and she graciously retreated saying she would put on some tea. So British.

Some changes occurred, in that Tony, who had trained as a jeweller, moved out to an apartment. I moved into his small bedroom and Michael moved his photographic business into my large bedroom. Michael and Joan took an apartment close by.

As the time came for me to leave school, there was the big question of what I was going to do. I hadn't a clue, but we got question papers from universities to see whether this route was feasible. We found I knew nothing of "Blake's dark satanic mills" or of obscure questions in algebra. I was practical and had some leanings toward buildings and construction. Perhaps this started on holiday with my mum in Pitlochry, Scotland when the engineer in charge of the new dam invited me down into its innards. I found this very interesting, walking through tunnels, seeing drills in action and men at work. Finally, with some outside advice, it was decided that I should study to be a chartered surveyor. I started work with A. Cobden Soar and Sons, chartered surveyors, on Victoria Street in London in 1948. My start was not auspicious since I arrived on my first Monday missing a front tooth, having had it cracked on the last day at school, Friday, while chasing my friend Peter Giffen. To have my tooth taken out, I was put under with gas.

I travelled an hour each day from Banstead to London. We worked a half day on Saturdays and could wear a sports coat on those days as opposed to a suit — a slight easing of the week's formality. The small company of eight was engaged in dealing with claims on war-damaged properties and valuing houses for mortgage purposes. Some days, one partner would take me in his Jaguar — what a delight! — to view properties to be valued. One morning, he came tearing in calling to me to get the Pharmaceutical Society on the phone. Disaster loomed when he found I was looking in the phone directory under "farmerseutical", followed by his complete denunciation of the current education system. In my first year, I studied by correspondence course and, by hard work, obtained my Preliminary Certificate, leaving an Intermediate and Final to pass to acquire professional membership. I liked the concept of a correspondence course because I could learn at my own speed. Shortly after this, I received my National Service call-up papers for the mandatory two years' military service required in Britain at that time, 1950. I could have delayed the service but decided to get it over with. Although it was fun in London and driving in my boss's car, the work did not seem to be going anywhere and would certainly not take me overseas. Perhaps I was still thinking about places like Switzerland.

CHAPTER 5

National Service
Germany
1950–1952

I passed a service medical and then received, with some apprehension, a rail pass to travel to Oswestry in North Wales where I was to join the Royal Artillery and become a gunner. On the train, I started identifying other recruits, and bonding started that lasted for the two years and beyond. On arrival, we were issued with all sorts of gear, and our civilian clothes were taken and returned to our homes. That night, in the barrack dormitory for twenty-four young rookies, this rapid transition from home life was too distressing for some who were crying. They had possibly never left home before. I just looked forward to what was going to happen in the coming days. Over the next two weeks, we were sorted out, given the elements of army drilling and marching along with frequent shouted orders by regular soldiers who probably despised us. I opted to train as a surveyor and after two weeks was transferred with some others by train to Larkhill Camp on Salisbury Plain about two miles from Stonehenge.

Here, over a six-month period, we were worked into physical shape and taught how to survey, drill, do guard duties, map read, strip and fire rifles and Bren guns and survive the idiosyncrasies of our sergeants, officers, and the army in general. The drilling produced some humorous moments — some recruits when doing an "about turn" started marching with their right arm forward together with their right leg. When we all acted together in unison, it seemed to be a moment of satisfaction to our officers and, I have to say, to us.

The purpose of our battery was to locate points from where enemy mortars were fired. Since they could be set up and fired from different places in a very short time, a retaliative response had to be found quickly. We would survey with four microphones about three hundred yards apart, opposite the probable area of mortar fire. When a mortar fired, the time of its sound wave hitting the microphones was recorded. With those three different times, we could calculate the co-ordinates of the mortar and report it to our own guns for retaliation. Therefore, our survey calculations had to be done at super speed using logarithmic tables. Since it was reckoned that the average life of a surveyor at the front was about 10 days, in reality it did not seem to be an effective system.

The rolling plains of Salisbury were fascinating, with their sweep of cultivated fields interspersed with woods, copses, farms tucked in at the bottom of slopes, and the extensive views with different blends of colours I could often see. Access to Stonehenge was not restricted in any way and became quite familiar, as we would regularly have to run up and around it and back to camp.

At the end of six months, we waited to learn where we would be posted permanently. Hong Kong? No thanks, since there was a rumour that one vaccination was a two-inch jab in the stomach and who wants that? Germany? All right for me, as it was interesting and close to home for leaves. Ten of us went to join the 115 Independent Locating Battery located in Dortmund, which was in the British Zone of Occupation. Germany was still occupied by the Russians, United States, and the French. As trained surveyors, we were the cream of the crop and received special treatment. This did not relieve the next one and a half years of boredom, compared to the first six months where we achieved fitness and learned a trade.

It seemed we were now just a statistical number to balance the various occupying forces. Some relief was obtained in sharpening our skills at surveying, learning sun and star shots, and participating in major maneuvers on Munster Lager Heath, north of Dortmund. Being in the bush and in the open instead of the barracks was a pleasant change, although the sight of massive tanks looming close by was a stimulus to digging your trench a lot deeper. In one important multinational maneuver, the equipment in our battery could not perform its job and officers were panicking until I suggested they change the cables and then it worked okay. For that I received a stripe to become lance-bombardier. It was extraordinary how this caused even guys I thought were friends to cheek me or push the limits whenever possible. To relieve the barrack-room boredom, we surveyors asked for the use of a truck so we could be dropped off in pairs around a pub some 8–10 miles away and hike and run in full gear to the pub using our maps to guide us. The earlier you arrived, the less you had to pay for the beer.

We also tried to learn German, although there was not a lot of motivation and certainly no direct order to keep attending lessons. In retrospect, we should have been made to learn the language. I used to meet up with young Germans and went on picnics with them or to the Mohair Zee dam, which British planes had bombed with innovative techniques during the war. Some senior Germans wanted me to teach them English and took me for a drive or beer while I corrected their English. Certain night clubs were out of bounds to troops who were not officers, but I would often put a German friend's raincoat on over my uniform and sneak in. It was a thrill to see another way of life inside, and I was always amazed at the minute size of the dance areas. Cigarettes and coffee were at a premium and were great for obtaining good bargains. Twenty cigarettes offered to the camp's German barber would get you a *fünfzig-fünfzig* (fifty-fifty) haircut instead of the regulation scalping. Even my girlfriend's father wanted cigarettes before he would let his daughter go out with me. What a cheek, but she was nice! And her name was Erika (Heather in English). Once I met her in the street with my uniform on instead of civilian clothes and she refused to walk with me, so that was the end of that. Tony told me that when he was first there, Germans would step off the pavement if a soldier was passing, a slight change of attitude.

We had to do guard duty in the camp. For this, twelve soldiers spivved themselves up with super-polished boots and creased trousers and lined up in order with rifles while an officer inspected them. The soldier looking the smartest got the evening off and the worst soldier got the job of supporting those on duty. When on maneuvers in the field, you were picked for two-hour shifts. Sometimes, in the winter, the extreme coldness would even penetrate my long johns, my army trousers, my work clothes, a heavy greatcoat, and a big ankle-length duffle coat. If somebody pushed me over, it was unlikely I could get to my feet. I just hoped I never fell over. It was also boring wandering around in the silent night, so I often opened our survey gear, got out a tripod and a theodolite, set them up, and studied the moon and the stars in the darkness.

Much of our time was spent playing cards, especially a solo game, for money. In our room of six, two could play bridge, and they taught the game and scoring to two of us. Our teachers would stand behind the learners to make sure we played the right cards (a good way to learn); the bidding was by the honour system and not by points, as it is now. On Sunday nights two of us often went down to a local *Ratskeller*, a basement-type pub, and drank beer while trying to talk with the locals. I got to a point where I could drink many beers and chasers of schnapps or *goldwasser*, and just manage to get back to the camp and off to sleep before nausea and sickness overcame me. One night in the winter, two of us were so busy drunkenly bowing each other onto the last tram (*strassenbahnwagon*) back to our camp (*Kaserne acht*) it moved off and left us running after it in our heavy greatcoats. We were late getting back into the camp, and officially absent without leave (AWOL). Fortunately, I had a good relationship with the sergeant in charge who said, "Get to your room quickly." Unfortunately, we ran into the sergeant-major who, as a penalty, restricted our use of civilian clothes during our last days in Germany, which was a bit of a pain. My earlier rise to the auspicious rank of lance-bombardier with its doubtful privilege was lost six weeks later for being absent without leave three times. Our company major said, "Now look 'ere 'ill. I've just about 'ad enough of you!" He did say on my demobilization card, "Hill will do a good job if so minded."

Perhaps that's part of my "do it now" outlook.

I think the pleasantest episode was when the battery went to Winterburg for a week's skiing holiday. While most of our group seemed to spend their time in the bars and clubs, four of us attended ski lessons in the morning, and then were taken in a bus to the top of the hill, and we skied back to the pub. I loved the speed of sliding over the snow and trying to control the direction by action on the skis. After lunch we were free, but would get our skis out again and hike up to where the bus had been and ski down in the afternoon. It was a wonderful experience after the drudgery of barrack life, and as some officers had their wives there, their presence made life seem a bit more normal again.

Back in the UK after the two years of National Service, I lived in our house in Norbury, south London as my mum had moved there from Banstead. My grandma lived there too, and Michael had his photographic business in one of the bedrooms.

Each year I had to do two weeks' army service for the next three years. I was assigned to the Honourable Artillery Company, the oldest regiment in the British Army. It dated back to 1537 when Henry VIII granted a charter to the Guild of Artillery of Longbows, Crossbows, and Handguns for "the better increase of the defence of this, our realm." Its premises were in the City of London. Sometimes I had to attend there or on a restricted heath for army maneuvers. Rather than being told to get on parade, I was always surprised to be asked, "Gentlemen, on parade, please." One evening, in these ancient guild quarters, a battle broke out in the mess between two sides, with officers riding on the backs of privates charging each other. I recall one colonel was wearing his ceremonial spurs!

On another occasion, we were shown a mass of vehicles and told, if we could drive, to take one and join a convoy to take them down to a camp. With the others, I ran like hell and grabbed a tracked Bren Gun carrier. I managed to get 55 mph out of it on the Portsmouth Highway and had great fun roaring over the rough heath during the two-week maneuvers.

CHAPTER 6

Meeting Heather
1952 onwards

With the end of National Service, I decided not to continue with the surveying course I had started. I was discussing this with an old friend from A. Cobden Soar and Son who suggested that the Polytechnic, Regent Street ran engineering courses over four years for diplomas, which qualified for professional membership in engineering institutions. This was a good suggestion, and I enrolled in civil engineering in 1952. And, whoopee, I obtained a staggering grant of 100 pounds a year. But I was teed off with this, as I found some foreign students got larger grants provided by England, and they had not spent two years in the army. In my first class of 40-odd students, there were three English guys (Peter Lawrence and Peter Chad were two good friends throughout) including me. The rest were from China (always top), Turkey, Armenia, Nigeria, Poland, Greece, and so on. I was always envious of those people who could absorb data when I had to drive it into my brain by repetition, or so it seemed to me. I would generally work six nights a week and two afternoons on the weekend.

In the army, I had lost track of several schoolfriends, so to find new friends, especially girls, I decided to take some dancing lessons. They proved quite useful and I thought Tuesday night would be my time to go to the Streatham Locarno dance hall to explore the marketplace. The hall had a big band on a raised platform on one side, an upper balcony all around the floor, couches and tables around the dance floor, and a snack place.

Spinning lights, which would be dimmed (hopefully) from time to time completed the scene. The girls without partners stood on one side of the entrance end of the floor and the boys stood on the other side. Others sat at tables. Picking a partner was a challenge. Perhaps this was the equivalent of today's online dating. If I asked one who was sitting down, she might be too tall or too small and even if the right height, she might not be able to dance. So, I watched for a while and then took the plunge. You were rarely turned down.

Some girls danced with considerable reserve and the occasional one with some abandon or even with the comment, "I bet you liked that." The evening might end with taking her home or at least getting her into a darker spot or obtaining a date for another time. With one girl I took home, we had to wait for her mum to go to bed. She finally gave in when I lit yet another cigarette. When alone, I happily helped the girl disrobe to the hips and, at my suggestion, she stood up, displaying herself in the moonlight, a rather exotic sight. Riding home furiously on my bike at three in the morning, I was stopped by the police, but they wanted my lights on. I was pretty lit up.

In my first summer vacation, I went as a student onto a major construction site for Dorman Long's new steel plant in Middlesbrough, Yorkshire, at two GBP a week. My bike was shipped up. On site, I had to check the "set" of each pile, to ensure they had been driven sufficiently far into the ground. This was a busy job as there were five rigs, each driving about five piles a day. One day, there was an urgent need to give a level for a concrete pour in a pit. When asked to provide it, I rushed over with my level and performed the task while the concreting crew and equipment were waiting. I really felt I was big time with the action involved, the smell of the site and the new concrete.

I enjoyed my six weeks there, especially meeting a local girl, Pauline, at a dance lesson and later hiking together many times across the sweeping slopes of the Yorkshire moors. We had a warm relationship and I loved being able to join in with her family life.

I got a valuable working lesson on my last day on the site. I was talking to the boss when a rig foreman came up and said they had driven a pile to its set, and would I check it? Since I was more interested in talking to the boss, I said, "Is the set correct?" He affirmed it was, so I said, "Okay, start the next pile." The boss blew his stack, believing that is how I had done my checking for the last six weeks. He marched over to the rig and had the set checked while we watched. The pile went down another inch, hardly anything, as did my reputation.

The next summer I got a union job in a printing shop through my mum, who still worked in the editorial department of the *Daily Express*. This meant sweeping the floors and cleaning the toilets, which I normally finished by 10 a.m., and was paid 14 GBP a week. Unions do have their uses. The foreman wanted to know how I could finish so quickly, and I was advised that to do this work, "Old Joe" used to require 20 minutes a day of overtime (so he could pick up an extra hour's overtime). I said, "I'm not Old Joe." I was horrified to find there were at least four or five tea breaks a day during which workers would play cards or darts that were available adjacent to their work areas. When I pointed out that there was no way they could be competitive in the marketplace, I received a visit from the foreman telling me to keep my mouth shut and my thoughts to myself. Later, workers would pass me on the stairs with a raised, clenched fist, perhaps as some sign of union solidarity.

During the Christmas holidays, I applied to work in the post office to help handle the extra load of post moving through. Sometimes I sorted letters into separate addresses or lobbed parcels across the room into open bags. With several temps doing this work it was fun, as they were often students and we all got on well together. And the money was good, better than when I worked as an engineering student on a site. In those days, it was said, with not earning money for four years as a student, it would take an engineer over 10 years to catch up money-wise with a labourer or tradesman. Not a motivating thought.

Pauline, my girlfriend, came down from Yorkshire for the next Christmas and survived the onslaught of my brothers' taunts about her cooking and habits. I think she was staggered, though, when we played the spoons game and all fought across the table when it was necessary to grab a spoon or be out. Before Pauline went home, we arranged we would go to Devon for a week in the summer, and I saw her off in London with many hugs.

Sometime later, my tennis friend called to say there was a tennis club dance coming up. I said I had had enough of them and wanted to use my time to study. He persuaded me to come, despite the extra study I needed to do for my degree, and he picked me up on his motorcycle. I think my stars were circling in a favourable orbit and I am eternally indebted to my friend for there, across the floor, was this 16-year-old girl in her low-cut gown, who immediately caught my attention more than any other in the room or on the dance floor. A rare spirit of calmness along with unusual beauty flowed from her. One look and I was lost, but dare I ask her for a dance? Yes, and as she rose and came into my arms, it seemed she might be keen as we wove round the floor to the music for the rest of the evening. Heather, who was still at school, says we met in a gentleman's excuse-me dance, but who am I to argue over this wonderful moment? I was a very lucky fellow.

When we were having refreshments, I particularly enjoyed asking her a question as she inhaled her cigarette through a long cigarette holder, the style of the day, which caused her no end of confusion deciding whether to answer the question first or breathe out the smoke. However, she agreed to come to a film on my next Tuesday night off, and I went home in high spirits. That Tuesday evening, there she was as I got on the same bus to go to the theatre, and I felt an electric jolt at this unexpected meeting. We saw Gregory Peck in the film *The Million Pound Note*. It was certainly worth every pound, and from then we met whenever we could between her tennis matches and tournaments and my studies. It took me five years before I took a set off her, and that was probably out of her kindness.

I was concerned about meeting Pauline again but continued with my plan to holiday with her. While waiting at the station for Pauline to get off the train for our holiday, my concern grew and I knew the instant I saw her, the interest was gone on my part.

This was an incredible reversal of the close relationship we had had. The warmth was lost. Our holiday was not the most pleasant interlude, unfortunately for her. I felt I killed her spirit when I told her my change of heart. At the house where we were staying, I had to explain our predicament to our young hosts and ask if we could have a refund if we left early; they kindly allowed this. I felt rotten that this had happened but a sense of relief that we were parting.

From then on, it seemed Heather and I could not see enough of one other, but it was four years before we were married. I do not remember any prepared build-up to my proposal because there was none. It seemed that one evening it just popped out and was accepted. This was certainly beyond "do it soon" and was definitely a "do it now" situation. (This was totally unlike our son, Jeremy's, proposal to his girlfriend, Ramy, when they landed on top of a snow-covered mountain in a helicopter. He proposed marriage, was accepted, and brought out champagne and glasses.) The day after my proposal when I came to Heather's house, I asked for a moment with her parents. I explained my love for Heather, that she had accepted me, and asked if they found that acceptable. They warmly agreed. Heather's younger brother, Roger, could hardly believe this was happening and looked staggered. My mum was especially pleased as she really liked Heather. When we asked a jeweller to look at daisy-cut engagement rings, he replied loudly and pompously, "That type is out of style," so we walked straight out and bought one elsewhere.

In the first of my two remaining summer vacations while studying, I hitchhiked to Switzerland to meet Heather, who had finished with her brother's school holiday group in Montreux. On the channel ferry, I met an artist who spent the trip sketching me. One of my lifts was along a German autobahn but, unfortunately, the driver turned off on a side road, leaving me on the autobahn, thumbing cars travelling at high speed. After two hours, none had stopped. As night was falling and there was a slight drizzle, things did not look too good in this isolated spot, when a motorcyclist came from the side turning and started to enter the autobahn. As he did, he glanced back at me and I quickly dropped to my knees with my hands up in a prayer motion. Thankfully, he motioned me to get on the pillion seat and thereafter I had the most hair-raising ride, drafting for two or three hours directly behind huge trucks and over cobbled streets. In Frankfurt, I virtually fell off his bike I was so cold and stiff but staggered away to get a train to Basel and Montreux. Later, Heather found me asleep on the floor where she was staying.

From there, we travelled across southern France to the Spanish border. In the early morning, standing by the road with our thumbs out, an open jeep with three guys picked us up, putting Heather in front and me in the back loaded down with luggage. Crossing through mountains and narrow valleys at Le Perthus and into Spain was a thrill. We got further lifts to Castelldefels, south of Barcelona. At that time, it was a more or less deserted beach with a couple of stores and a dance place behind. A German couple with a large tent on the beach said we could use it while they were away for a few days. I said to Heather, "How lucky can we get?" The sea was warm and the beach perfect. Then, with money beginning to run short, we made our way up through Pamplona to San Sebastian, Paris, and home. It was a wonderful trip, exploring life together with Heather, experiencing rides with all kinds of people and accepting their hospitality.

Hitchhiking had its ups and downs but was always interesting. I might be thumbing for an hour only to see a car stop, two girls with short shorts jump out, run forward, and hitch the next car, while I was still left thumbing. With Heather it was easier, but sometimes a big truck might slow down to pick Heather up but suddenly, seeing me, speed up again. Once, we had just left a lift in a cement truck when the next car, flying a Spanish ensign, stopped. The driver must have been the local state's head guy because as we passed people in the villages, they doffed their hats or Guardia Civil men would present arms; we just waved royally from the back seat.

One evening, sitting beside an empty road wondering if we would get a lift, a couple returning from farming their fields made signals inviting us to stay the night. As the wife had such an infectious laugh, we had a fine evening despite the language barrier. On another day, as a truck came towards us, I was sure the front wheels occasionally left the road, as the balance of the load was so bad. I said to Heather, "Do we want to risk this?" She said, "Yes," and the three guys invited us into the front. A short while later, all the reinforcing steel fell off the back. We got out, laughing with them, and helped to reload it. The drivers took us to their favourite restaurant, introduced us to *paella*, a most edible dish, and showed us how to drink wine with the bottle spout six inches from our mouths. We never knew what the next event might be, and that was the fun of the whole experience.

On a lift into Paris from Marseille, a couple ran out of money so we lent them what we had left to buy petrol. On arrival, their friends repaid us, and they dropped us off at a police station where we stayed the night. At a nearby restaurant we held our money out to the waiter telling him, "This all the money we have." He treated us royally and actually provided a bottle of wine.

As an aside, when our daughter, Erica, went hitchhiking in Europe on her own, she did not have such a happy time, as she was harassed by a policeman in a train compartment while a woman there did nothing. In an Italian youth hostel, guys were knocking on her door all night. She had no problem when her brother Jeremy joined her.

Back in England we were always out hiking or travelling somewhere. Once when in a train going to Brighton, it stopped in the middle of some woods full of bluebells. I said to Heather, "Do we really want to go on to Brighton with all the crowds on the beach or shall we jump out right here?" She immediately said, "Yes, let's jump." Were we beginning to think in parallel? We quickly opened the compartment door, jumped down beside the track, slammed the door, and ran down the bank and over the fence into the woods, followed by the angry shouts of the train guard.

It was about this time that Heather had won her way through 16 rounds of tennis to become a finalist in the London Parks Tournament. The rounds were played against winning opponents in various parks — a challenging feat. The final was played on a clay court at the famous Wimbledon Tennis Club, which was pretty exciting. When Heather lost the first set and was down 5–3 in the second, I had already smoked half my weekly cigarette allowance. Finally, she got into her rhythm, which can be deadly, retrieved the second set and went on to win the third set. Her parents and I cheered madly, and I still had some cigarettes left. Many years later, when Heather was 65 and 70, she was asked to play tennis for Canada in Turkey and Australia, respectively, and afterwards played in the following Open Tournaments. I am very proud of her coloured jackets with CANADA on the back. In 2018, she was again asked to play for Canada in Croatia, where her team came third.

Heather's parents were very progressive and trusting of me to let their young and only daughter come on our hitchhiking trips. Heather's mum's only comment was that if we were going to get married, they would like to be there. I must have seemed serious about marrying her. Heather's family was the first I had ever met where the children called their parents by their Christian names. They were also the first people I knew who had a TV, albeit with a six-inch screen.

Our second trip was hitchhiking through France to Menton and down to Venice, coming back over the Saint Bernard Pass in Switzerland. We found Venice with its many waterways, narrow passages and wonderful architecture to be an extraordinary city. Our early morning strolls through the back alleys, over little bridges across small waterways with the early morning shadows and sunlit areas was so different from anything else we had seen. One day, we paid a valuable two pounds and took a trip on a gondola. The gondolier delighted us as he started singing while stroking along. The scene developed into a romantic moment when a window above opened and a woman looked out and started singing with him. We blew kisses to her as we passed. It was an extra special treat to remember.

CHAPTER 7

Engineering Study
1952–1956

During my long years of study, when I had met Heather and become engaged, there were many occasions when I wondered if the study was all worth it, and times when I queried the relevance of subjects to my course in civil engineering. Sometimes I read a magazine during a chemistry lesson, but there were also good times when I seemed to absorb and understand everything a professor talked about. In our mechanical work lessons, the teacher said he could play hoopla with my lathe work, and I responded, "I am not physiologically suited for that type of work."

However, subjects really became interesting in the last two years when we studied planning, design of concrete and steel structures, costing and management. I felt I was beginning to get somewhere I wanted to go. Groups started working together and results came a lot more easily. Last minute cramming for exams was exhausting, but at the same time it was satisfying that I could motivate myself to absorb and remember so much. Being threatened by certain foreign students if I did not pass along answers during the exams was also a new experience. The final exam period consisted of ten exams over six workdays and concluded successfully.

During my studies, I took buses each day to get up to the Regent Street Polytechnic or even bicycled to and fro. Because it was such an effort, I bought a motorcycle for the trip. My brother Tony used to buy and sell motorcycles, and I loved the slow putt-putt tick-over of his 250cc Triumph and the muffled low purr of his Francis Barnett motorcycle. When I told him what I was going to buy, he suggested I ask a seller if the sprockets were worn. At that question the seller said, "You tell me what a sprocket is, and I'll tell you if it's worn!" It was another lesson in life, especially when Tony later commented, "I wouldn't give you 10 pounds for it!" But I did get 10 pounds for it, later. It had its moments, but Heather and I had fun on it. Once we were cheered by a crowd when, during the Old Crock's race from London to Brighton, it just made it up a hill. When leaving Heather's house late in the evening, the kick-start would often make a startling bang in the quietness of her cul-de-sac. On the colder days I wore my army greatcoat, and Heather loved the lingering odour. I took her mum for a ride once, and as we went round bends, I would lean inwards, but she would lean outwards, making us look like some trick team. Even my mum tried one while waiting at a bus stop for her trip to London. A motorbike rider offered her a lift and she hopped on even though she was wearing a skirt.

When I received my results after all the years of study, I leapt with glee, hugged my mum and later Heather. A great load had been lifted off my shoulders and I felt I could move onto the next step, earning money and being an engineer. I had reached a new plateau, and an incredible feeling of relief flowed through me.

A few interviews led to starting my engineering career at Simon Carves under Charles Reynolds, author of many books on concrete technology. The project was the design of two nuclear power stations. Working in a busy design office, I was concerned at the chaos and disturbance that was tolerated. I used to protest frequently to no avail. Although the design work was interesting, within six months I decided to emigrate to Canada. This massive "do it now" decision was prompted by two experiences. Once, standing on Norbury station platform with a crowd of passengers, I heard that the train (which I could then afford) would be late — a frequent occurrence. I swore, and a man beside me said, "I have been doing this for seven years." I replied, "I'm not going to." The second experience involved my student friend, Peter Chadd, telling me he was going to emigrate to Canada. I said that sounded interesting, and he invited me to his apartment one night to discuss his plans.

As the evening wore on, with another beer or two, the whole concept became quite tangible, attractive and feasible. Not only would it be different, a new challenge, but all the mountains and coastline in the west looked interesting. Peter and I even thought we might make money there and return after a couple of years. The key issue for me was that I had lived at home and in the army and had never supported myself. Further, I wanted to see if I liked Canada and could survive there. After some discussion with Heather, I said I wanted to go on my own for six months to ensure I could support us both when we got married. Fortunately for me, she agreed.

Not having much money after four years of study, we wanted to make sure we were going to like this radical change of environment. We had read and heard about immigrants returning from Australia when the government had paid for their ten-pound passage to go there because they had not liked it. Rumours circulated that it was difficult to find work in Canada and that it was a cold place. That didn't concern me as millions of people lived there. A number of people criticized my leaving England after having taken advantage of the money for my training. My workmates approved and gave me a farewell present of two signed technical books and wished me success — a nice and much appreciated send-off.

I passed the medical test required, but there was a scary moment as I was requested to return for a second X-ray for TB. I let out a sigh of relief when I learned the first one had not come out properly. I was concerned, as Michael was being treated for TB. He smoked too much. When I went back to get my final papers from Canada House in November 1956, there was a huge line-up around the block caused mainly by the start of the Suez Crisis, and people wanting to leave Britain. In simple terms, the crisis was caused by Egypt's Sadat nationalizing the canal and forcing the British who had controlled it to leave. In fact, for the next five or six years, over 200,000 people emigrated from Britain to Canada each year, about 90% of Canada's intake during that time.

Our parents, family and friends encouraged us to go. I think at that time many people found England still run-down and emigration to another country was a kind of release, with perhaps more opportunities.

CHAPTER 8

First View of Canada,
Marriage
1956–1957

My mum had managed to get me a passage as a supernumerary in one of the four cabins on board a ship called the SS *Caslon*. The *Daily Express* was owned by Lord Beaverbrook, a Canadian, and received its paper from St. John, New Brunswick in small freighters. It would be leaving from Glasgow, and likely be free. I took it immediately.

Later, when I was close to emigrating to Canada, my mum showed me around the back streets of London to remind me what I was leaving behind. We might just turn off the main street and down some narrow walkway I had not seen before and into the Inner Temple square with quiet gardens and cloisters away from the roar of London's traffic, or to the Sherlock Holmes pub, certain churches and Bridewell Theatre. Although her other three sons were close to her, I think my departure was a sad wrench as Michael thought I was her favourite son. In a way, I think Heather was my replacement while I was in Canada, as they had outings together, including going to film reviews.

Heather decided to come with me up to Glasgow to see me off to Canada. It reduced our separation by a couple of days, and I was so pleased she came with me and saw the ship. We left from a cold and smoky St. Pancras railway station, as our families waved goodbye after many hugs and a few tears. I'm sure my mum held on tight to her emotions as we had a last hug. I felt sorry for her knowing she would essentially be alone in our Norbury house with my grandma. The train slowly pulled away from the platform and we waved our last farewells. A man who had been standing close by at an open window in the train corridor had heard our goodbyes and realizing our situation, said he was also going to Glasgow and kindly offered us his own overnight sleeping compartment. Now there was a rare type with empathy. Just how fortunate can you get?

In the darkness of the early morning hours, the train completed its rocking and noisy trip and we disgorged into Glasgow station, finding it as dirty as the one we had left. Being rather early to board, we explored parts of the worn-down looking town on a bus as we clung close to keep warm, knowing our time together was diminishing quickly. I'm sure the conductor thought we were mad, or at least odd, not knowing where we wanted to go. In his strong Glasgow accent, he asked, "Where to?" and we replied, "To the last destination and back."

I cannot remember if he rolled his eyes or shook his head at this request. We probably didn't look part of the scene, either. In this area of town, it seemed we were accompanied by men in working clothes who needed to cough and spit so much we wondered if they were all miners. It was not a pleasant interlude, but we were in our bubble of love. Later, after we saw the freighter I was to take, I took Heather back to the train station where we really did have our last farewell hugs, kisses and promises for a while.

As I walked back along this dreary, drab brick dock area, lined with old cranes and railway lines, grey clouds swirled overhead and strong gusts threatened my balance. It was two weeks before Christmas, and I was trying to stay warm in my light Raglan raincoat, even with its detachable woollen lining. As I plodded toward my ship, I experienced a mixture of sadness and excitement. Sadness because I had just enjoyed my last warm closeness to Heather as she boarded a train back to her home in Mitcham, south of London, and excitement, as I was heading for a new adventure. I was going to take a freighter to Canada for six months, as an immigrant, before I returned so we could get married. That was hoping we were still on the same wavelength, and that she had not found some guy who drove out all the wonderful ties and pleasures we had experienced over the four years we had been together. Six months was going to seem like a very long time. Was I still going to be the same and have the same feeling for Heather?

Now, as I approached the 5,300-tonne ship, it looked enormous, dark, and efficient with its on-deck handling gear, single red funnel, and large bridge with lines running everywhere. Little did I know that later in life I would be the development manager for a port in Chile to handle and load massive 250,000-tonne iron ore freighters.

I slowed as I came to the ship's gangway and as my hand grasped the handrail, I looked across the length of *my* ship for the next two weeks and had the sudden realization that I was about to step into another world. I was about to leave my English life of 24 years behind. How would I react to all the new experiences? A shiver of excitement and apprehension surged through me as I imagined the new adventures I might encounter.

At the top of the gangway, I was welcomed by a crew member who called for one of the officers to show me to the cabin that would be my home for the trip. He then gave me a tour of the areas I could use, although I was free to wander over the ship. The trip took 14 days, and luckily, I had twelve seasick pills and managed to survive the winter gales.

The two-week trip in the middle of winter was at times a wild experience. Thank heavens for the pills, which quelled my worst nausea. I spent much of my time on the bridge, listening to how they operated and navigated the ship by sextant readings as there was no GPS. Being winter, there were times when this small ship crashed forward into one sizable wave after another, and spray smashed and rattled on the bridge windows. Certain windows had revolving circular glass sections which threw the water aside and provided a clear view forward. The whole hull was vibrating as if it was being shaken by some monster hand. I could feel the movement through my feet. As an engineer, I found the experience disturbing and wondered how the ship designers could take into account the forces that the steel structures were being subjected to by the vibrations. The forces were strong enough to make the captain and crew curse from time to time.

Being the only passenger, I could eat in the officers' mess at the captain's table. He was a Geordie with a strong accent from Tyneside in northeast England, and it took me three or four days before I could grasp what he said. I wondered if my grandfather had the same accent. Sometimes I played bridge with the captain, the first officer, and the chief engineer, which helped pass the time. Most of the day, I read or spent time on the bridge discovering how the first officer calculated where the ship was by taking sun-shots. Crew members might come by for a chat about their plans, girlfriends and happenings on the boat. Of course, we had a traditional Christmas dinner on board, but afterwards all the officers and I had to go into the galley and serve up dinner to the deck crew. With the violent motion of the ship, the scene in the galley was utterly chaotic as utensils, food, cutlery, and anything loose slid across counters or fell on the floor while we tried to keep our footing and fill the plates.

On my last night, as the ship ghosted into Port St. John on New Year's Eve 1956-7, I remember slipping onto the bridge, noticed by the captain but allowed to stay. It was an impressive sight standing on the darkened bridge, watching the slow movement of the ship amid the maze of coloured navigation lights; I wondered what they all meant. It eased into the dock and lines were thrown ashore. Finally, she was berthed. It was time to go.

I thanked the captain, said goodbye to the crew, picked up my suitcase and walked down the gangway to the railway station and my next experience. It was −22 degrees Fahrenheit and mighty cold, colder than anything I had experienced. My ears were frozen and my rain-jacket seemed porous. I paid the train fare from my meagre $75. Being New Year's Eve, the train to Toronto with its open carriages was nearly empty, but I got talking to a girl who told me there were rooms available where she stayed near downtown Toronto. It was a relief knowing where I could go when I arrived.

The boarding house had ten boarders, and the rooms and location were good. I was made very welcome and within a week

I had an engineering job at $330 a month. Knowing English engineers in Toronto were getting $400 per month, I argued for that, but the boss man said, "If you can get that, take it. But if you can't, come back and I will hire you." I came back. I was impressed by the size of the office, the industrious way people worked, the fixed coffee break, and that they all seemed to wear similar partially transparent nylon shirts with white T-shirts underneath. I was put to work immediately.

As soon as possible I bought skis and on the weekends a group of us, maybe three or four in the front and four or five in the rear seat of a huge car (all cars seemed huge and had no seat belts) drove on Friday nights up the 401 highway with country music blasting out, sometimes in a snowstorm. Huntsville was our usual stop where we stayed in log cabins. After supper, we indulged in square dancing while one man played his fiddle, which he held across his lap. He would play late into the night until we dropped. During the night, in our dormitory room, a watchman came in and fed more logs on the fire, but we were generally too tired to notice. This was a whole new world.

My landlady often took pity on my two-burner meals and brought up to my room a welcome wholesome home-cooked dinner. My evening entertainment was generally studying up for some problem I had to deal with in the office the next day, reading *Doctor Zhivago*, or writing a letter to Heather. Later, I shared the upper two rooms with an ex-policeman from England who loved to cook, leaving me to clear up. I took over from his roommate, Alan Osborne; Alan and I are still in touch. In fact, he recently called to tell me his wife, Pearl, had just passed away. I invited him to visit us anytime. Occasionally, with friends I had made, we went out in the evening and had drinks in a hotel bar at the top of some high-rise building — a completely new experience making me think this was the life!

After two months, my boss asked if I wanted to work at a steelwork's in Sault Ste. Marie, 500 miles north. I went the next week and was impressed by the sheets of ice over Lake Huron, as I took my first-ever flight. The whiteness of the iced-up lakes below was stunning compared to the blackness of the watercourse where ships had broken through. I was travelling with a German colleague, and when the stewardess was bending over to serve drinks across the aisle, I was astounded but amused to see him lean across and make out that he was going to bite her rather well-rounded and attractive derriere. Later, when I got to know him, I took his family out for a drive. This Teutonic engineer told his wife to thank me for the drive; he did not. You never know what people are really like.

I was lodged at the Windsor Hotel, where I had a great view of the Soo locks and the continual movement of Laker ships passing through them. Often, when there was ground fog, I could only see the upper structure of the moving ships. In those days, it was said that more tonnage passed through these locks during the eight months of the year they were open than through the Panama and the Suez Canals combined.

Sault Ste. Marie, or the Soo, was my introduction to small town Canada; it was always different and interesting. Late on Fridays and Saturdays, there were cars roaring up and down the main street filled with the youths of the town leaning out the windows, banging on the car doors, and shouting out to girls. Now and then, I had an invitation from my new boss to go to the local ice hockey game against, say, North Bay. Drinking in the hotel bar was a standard social time where, during the course of many beers, each noted with a pencil mark on your beer mat, not-so-good looking women soon became pretty attractive.

In cafes, I found coffee served with a small plastic packet of real cream. It was so delightfully rich, I once asked the waitress for a full glass of cream, and she stated very firmly, "You mean milk?" I replied, "No, the cream you have for coffee," and with a look of complete disbelief and with a rising voice, she said, "You really want a whole glass of real cream?" I was hoping she would keep her voice down as customers were looking interested. With a hopeful look, I said, "Yes, please," to which her reply in an exasperated tone was, "I don't know what I would charge you." It was a nice, decadent drink after the austerity of England.

Rationing had only just stopped in 1954, and the economy was still weak as it recovered from the war.

My room on the fifth floor, the highest I had ever lived, had a view across the town below and across the Canadian and American locks, but the water radiator heating system provided a number of hammer blows, I could have well done without. The acoustic torture would often start, usually at night, with a kind of rattling sound growing in intensity until there was a thundering crash and then it would go quiet until the pressure built again. I eventually had my room changed.

On another occasion, there was a hammering on my door in the middle of the night. A friend was shouting, "Get up, Patrick! The smelt are running." Through the fog of sleep, I considered what smelt might be, why were they running, and where the hell were they running to at night? After an hour of driving in inky blackness, the countryside was suddenly lit by a multitude of car lights focused on a small river, and my questions were answered. What a scene! People were crowding into the river and collecting full buckets of the small fish — a rare experience for a rookie-come-lately to Canada. Some fires were going where the fish were being cooked.

For my six months away, there was a continual flow of letters between Heather and me. The important one, which set me on fire, occurred when she told me our wedding date had been set, and she and my mum had started making arrangements for the big day. That was good news and now I could make detailed plans to return home. I suggested to Heather we would work in Montreal when we came back. The other many hot letters to Heather now live somewhere in a home cupboard and are hopefully never found. Although my children might disown me if they ever got to read them, the revealing text of many published books suggests they might make a fortune. I really must have a final read of the yearnings of the day and then burn them.

With the job finished, I left the Soo for the long drive back to Toronto and had another experience, but not so pleasant. Rolling down a more or less deserted and lonely forest-lined road in my newly purchased V8 1947 Mercury "monster" car (my $200 wedding present for Heather when she returned with me to Canada in four weeks' time), a pick-up truck with two guys inside caught up and pulled alongside me at 60 mph. This was worrying as they stayed alongside for a while looking at me, then pulled across in front of me and slowed right down causing me to slow. Uh-oh, I thought, what's the game here? Not a happy situation. It left me no option but to pull out, overtake, and resume my original speed. The same thing happened again — they came alongside looking at me, pulled in front, and again slowed down. This was starting to look serious and like something I had never experienced. Road rage had not surfaced yet as a driving feature. I did not like this at all. It was quite frightening, there being no one else around, so, on pulling out this time, I floored the gas and roared away until I got to the next town. In Toronto, I quit my job, picked up my belongings and drove up to Montreal. My few days there proved it would be an interesting place to live so I left the car on an empty lot and flew back to England.

At home, the vicar at the Streatham Parish Church said I was a fortunate man as Heather and my mum had made all the arrangements for the wedding, posting the banns, sending out invitations, etc. and, of course, he was right. Some 200 relatives and friends attended, many of whom were from Heather's tennis club. It was a top hat, Moss Brothers affair for the key males, which I strongly resisted until taken aside by my cousin Valerie's husband, an architect, who persuaded me to change my mind, saying this was a big day for the bride.

There had not been much time for a rehearsal at the church so during the service the super vicar would mutter, "Come a bit closer," from time to time so he could direct us properly. When he knelt, there was a hole in his right shoe. Finally, Raymond, who was pleased to be my best man, handed me the ring, which I slid onto Heather's finger and we were married on 13 July 1957. On leaving the church, confetti descended on us as we headed for the reception. This was more than just a wedding but a farewell, which justified some of the 200 guests.

Within an hour of leaving the wonderful reception and dance, all superbly organized by Heather's parents and their friends, Tony's car, which he had lent us, was in a ditch after we had been racing another car. Our honeymoon in Devon, with Heather's red almost transparent nightie, was an adventurous seven days ending with our sending a telegram to Michael to forward some money as we could not fully pay for the place we were staying at, in Lulworth Cove. One of Heather's parents' moneyed friends said we *must* stay at this *marvellous* hotel on a cliff top. As we stopped and opened the car doors, a gust swept confetti into the entrance. Having arrived rather late, we confirmed dinner was still being served. After perusing the menu, we ordered from the formal waiter. When he finally brought the food, we noticed it was not what we had ordered. When we protested, he replied, "That's all that's left." We took it without complaint.

Back home, where we kindly had the use of Michael and Joan's apartment, we packed all we owned, mainly clothes and books and our wedding gifts, into tea chests and trunks. This time at the departure station, there were sad goodbyes from Heather's parents and my mum and wishes for good luck. Heather was quite sad her father had, for some reason, not been able to make it to the station on time. Although we were excited, I'm sure our parents wondered whether they would see us again. As the train whistle went there were last-minute shouts and waves as we slowly moved out of the station on our way to Liverpool where we were to catch the *Corinthia* to Montreal. Charlie O'Reilly was our porter who manhandled our gear through the boarding process. Seven days later, we woke up to see a tyre fender outside our porthole. We had arrived in Canada, August 1957.

CHAPTER 9

"Back in Canada, eh?"
1957–1962

Our first task was to find the deserted car lot where I had left my car. There it was looking rather melancholy, dusty, and with three flat tyres. Heather said, "The engagement ring was better." After getting the tyres fixed, we bought a local newspaper and drove around searching for a place to live. We took a room in a large house where we shared a kitchen and two bathrooms with thirteen young people, apparently all immigrants. We took it because we had little money and no jobs. It had its funny moments like when Gretchen Billesberger, one half of a German couple, told us she had been "cooking" her husband Billy's shirts.

With her legal background, Heather managed to get a job with an insurance company fairly quickly and I got an engineering job with Canada Pacific Railway in the design office at Windsor railroad station. As the money trickled in, we opened a bank account and started looking around for a better place with our own facilities. We found a cozy place and moved out with the Billesbergers to share several rooms. After two or three months, we had made several friends and took them exploring in our monster car with maybe four in the front and five in the back. It was good to have friends with us as we often had to push to get it started. In our first week it broke down in town and I had to get help, while Heather had the new experience of directing Quebec traffic around it — people were not too courteous.

As our funds grew, we bought skiing equipment for Heather, and before winter arrived, we decided to sell the monster. After approaching several car lots to sell it, where we dared not stop the engine lest we couldn't start it, someone offered us $25, which we quickly took with our "do it now" outlook, and dined out that night after taking a bus home. I had paid $200 for it and surprisingly later saw it parked on our street! I asked the guy sitting in it, "Does this car clonk in reverse gear?" Looking surprised he said, "Yes," and added he had paid $150 for it.

We later bought a much smaller English Hillman car, which also had a bench seat in the front, so we could still, in a pinch, get eight friends in it but only friendly friends because it was very squishy. We drove all over the place to the Laurentians for skiing and picnics at St. Agathe, Christabel, St. Saveur, and down into the New England states. One of the problems in the Laurentians was that all the lakes seemed to be surrounded by private property, meaning we had to trespass to get a swim — a lesson for any urban or rural planner.

Although good friends with Billy and Gretchen, we now decided we wanted a furnished apartment with a bedroom, lounge, kitchen and bathroom for ourselves and we found one with a balcony on Clairmont Ave., Westmount. It had a trash chute on our floor where trash could be dropped down into the basement. I could get a train from Attwater station nearby, and it took me right into Windsor station where I worked. One day on the train I met Vic May, an Aussie accountant, and we were pleased to find we both lived in the same apartment building, he with his wife, Eve. She was an amateur opera singer, a flamboyant blonde who would arrive formally dressed at a casual evening party, or in minimal shorts at a more formal evening. Later we met Scottish Joe, a carpet salesman, and his wife Margaret, a fun couple who lived on the floor below us.

Being in a new cultural environment was exciting because of the people with their French and different immigrant accents when speaking, dressing and behaving; the huge cars, buses, and tram systems; music; high-rise buildings; the duplexes with outside stairs down to the street from their upper floors; the cold winter and humid summer; double doors in all commercial buildings to keep the heat in along with double frame windows. I had a problem addressing my boss by his Christian name, not a habit in England. Generally, we had no need to speak French as most people spoke English. Sometimes, though, since I had a beard, unusual in those days, a passerby might mutter, "'esus Christ?"

The newness and difference of life was always surprising, certainly as winter approached. We had to buy overshoes because of the snow and slush. I was amused at the number of overshoes that appeared out of snow piles as they melted. Heavier clothes were required. Heather had to take ski lessons. She learned how to use a tow rope and not fall off when others were coming up behind her, who would have to step off if she could not get up and get going again. I'd have to tie up her lace boots because her hands were too cold. When we heard "Snow Clearance" shouted out in our building, we had to tear out and move our car to another street before the snow clearance vehicle dumped a pile of snow on it that would require one or two hours to move before getting the car out. Of course, one had to buy a *wood* shovel to do that to avoid scratching the paint. French Canadians kindly invited us to their summer cottage or cabin and we were given corn cobs to eat, a first for us. They were curious why we had never eaten one before. They also invited us to parties, some pretty rowdy, where we just sat around drinking beer from cans. In our first Christmas, Heather bought a 25lb turkey; did she think I needed building up? We couldn't get it in the oven, and I'm sure we had turkey sandwiches and soup for the following month.

As well as having a bedroom, we had a pull-down bed in the living room wall cupboard, which was good because it was by the balcony door and gave us a good breeze on a hot night. One night, when we came in late, being a bit under the weather, I just dropped my clothes in the bedroom, did not put any lights on, ran round into the room, and dived onto the bed. As I crashed onto the floor, I realized that Heather had closed it up before going to work!

Sometimes we took a fast drive up Mount Royal hill if there was not too much snow. If there was, we might walk across the Jacques Cartier Bridge and look at the snow and ice piled up on the St. Lawrence River and feel the shake of the bridge from vehicular traffic. We learned later that when the manual toll was changed to an automatic toll, some 20% more money was taken. As spring came around, we took trips over the border into the New England states, the Adirondack hills, New York, Boston, New Hampshire, Vermont, Maine, went skiing at Sugar Loaf, and even at Tuckerman Ravine, Mount Washington, which has recorded the highest wind speed of 240 mph. We loved the look of the long-established countryside, towns and villages whereas Quebec had a somewhat raw look in comparison and was smothered in billboards.

We started to learn that Quebec was a have-not province and was subsidized mainly by Ontario, Alberta, and British Columbia; the federal government wanted Quebec's strong voting power. We also started to hear that in rural areas if you did not turn up for church you could get a visit from a priest enquiring whether there was a problem. If you did not turn up again, you might find difficulty in being served at the local shops. True or not I do not know, but I did know that I had to tip to get served in turn when buying a sandwich at the station lunch counter.

Back on the work scene, Heather was faring well with the Standard Life Insurance, but I was getting bored with the limited design opportunities and lack of fieldwork. I was surprised to find a man who worked there who had actually been with the Canadian troops close to the station at Ashtead where I had been evacuated. However, CPR had some odd arrangements. Firstly, we were paid every two weeks. When the accountant came round with the pay envelopes, he bypassed me, saying they withheld the first week's pay, but at the next payout I would get two week's pay. When I asked how I was supposed to live without pay for three weeks, my boss said he would give me a loan. Well, it was not a loan as he took me to a bank and stood as guarantor while I borrowed the money. Another issue came at holiday time when I put my name down for my two weeks' holiday and I was told I could only have one week as I had not worked a full year in the preceding year. To this I said, "I have worked a year here and I need my appropriate rest period," but this was not accepted.

So I found out how many employees worked in the company and calculated how much extra money the company was making from the withholding process. I wrote to the CEO, Mr. Crump, explained my complaint, and said it was unreasonable that they were making nearly a million dollars a year out of us. The basic reply was, if you don't like it, move on. This I did.

Within a short time, Heather and I left our companies, cancelled our apartment, and loaded our car to the hilt with Joe and Margaret, handing final items in through the windows to go on Heather's lap. It was September 1958, and we intended to drive across the US to Vancouver. It was late in the year as we headed off through Toronto, Detroit, Chicago, Iowa, and South Dakota to pass through the Badlands.

It's difficult to appreciate the size of this country when flying across, but on the third day of driving across the rolling prairies, I found it difficult to stay awake at 10 in the morning. The road stretched interminably to the far horizon, which was topped by a big, blue sky vista dotted with bulging white cumulous clouds. And, at the end of the trip, I knew we had only crossed half the country. Much of the time we seemed to be the only car around as the miles rolled ahead. Occasionally, I would pull off at the side of the road, drop the seat back, and have a ten-minute *kip* or nap to reinvigorate — a habit I had learned in the army.

As we closed in on the Badlands, we started singing a song that seemed appropriate to the country we were coming into:

'Hang down yer head, Tom Dooley
Hang down yer head and cry.
Hang down yer head, Tom Dooley
Poor boy, y'are bound to die.'

Viewed from the road, the grandeur of the park with its many peaks was quite spooky in the evening light. Heather firmly stated she did not want to camp out there. The rounded and irregular peaks of stratified rocks with their dull colours did not look attractive.

We managed to find an open motel as most were closed, it being late in the season. We had just settled back on the bed, wondering where we could get something to eat, when there was knock on the door. A man standing there with a bottle of rye whisky suggested we might like a drink before dinner. We invited him in as he said, "My mum, who owns the motel, does not approve of my drinking so I thought I'd slip up to your cabin." He was the CEO of a soap manufacturing company in St. Louis, Missouri, and was visiting his mum. After a few drinks, he said, "Come on down to the kitchen in 20 minutes, and I'll have supper ready for you." The supper was braised pheasant with mushrooms plus a touch of sherry followed by a simple dessert — a tasty meal we had not expected, which was much appreciated.

The next day we had a better look at the impressive Badlands but saw no bison. We passed through Wyoming, across the rolling slopes of Montana and up to Calgary. Sitting in a bar in Montana, Heather had a splendid shock. She saw her first cowboy push through the double swing doors. A tall, lean, well-built guy strode in, dressed in black with his cowboy hat on. I think she breathed a little more heavily.

In Calgary, we were surprised to see the peaks of snow-covered mountains on the horizon. Instead of immediately looking for work, we took a drive to Banff and were overwhelmed by the massive surrounding vistas. We thought we would stay on for a winter, but I could not find a job in Calgary, so we headed up to Edmonton, where I was able to get a job with the provincial highways department. We found lodgings in an old house downtown and we were set for the winter.

We couldn't believe how cold it was. It peaked at minus 35°F, and with wind chill, touched minus 67°F. Walking to work was a freezing process and probably explained why the offices were heated to some 80°F. Many car stalls had electric outlets so you could plug the block heater in to keep the engine warm.

Driving off in the morning, you might find the car bumping along for a while because the part of the tyres in contact with the ground had frozen flat. The clear blue skies would often give the impression of a nice warm day, but we weren't deceived — that meant it was colder than usual. We even played bowls in the apartment with frozen apples or oranges that were left overnight in the car.

Even our apartment was cold despite the oil heater with its octopus-like distribution arms located in the basement. It was a real fire hazard. One day, and only once, I complained to the landlord that our place was cold. He said, "I'll be over in 30 minutes." When I opened the door, he was carrying a machine on his shoulder with saw teeth. I quickly learned this was a chainsaw as he walked over to the side of the room and pulled a line on the machine, which started up with an ear-splitting roar. He then neatly cut a one-foot square hole in the floor against the wall over the basement where the furnace was, saying, "That should fix it. You should be okay now." A landlord of action!

Heather got an interesting job as a legal secretary for a QC, but at my office I found work rather boring. Some fifteen engineers, each using an adding machine, were calculating cut and fill earth volumes from cross-sections on rolls of graph paper showing road sections that were to be built when the winter was over. The only entertainment occurred when a rather shapely secretary could be heard walking down the hall and coming into our room. As she did this, the clatter of the adding machines would ease to a stop. Did she realize each arrival cost the department about $150, at least by my calculations?

I still had my beard and one day somebody in the office told me my wife was waiting outside at reception for me. Wondering what had happened to Heather, I went outside to find a local Mennonite woman dressed in black with a black shawl over her head. I laughed at this trick, but I did not laugh at a serious interlude with our office manager that occurred in the spring. Calling me into his office one day, he asked, referring to my beard: "Do you wear 'that' for medical or religious reasons?"

Shocked at his rather offensive and abrupt attitude, I replied, "I wear it because I like it."

Incredibly, his aggressive response was: "I don't like it and I want it off."

I wondered if he was some kind of control freak, and realizing the ramifications of my reply, "I don't actually recall asking you for your opinion," would mean all hell breaking loose, I was proved right.

However, I felt I was on safe ground, as the two head engineers had interviewed me without comment and I was intending to leave in any case. Imagine that happening these days!

Socially we found people were very friendly, but when we left our apartment on New Year's Eve to go out for a drink and join in the fun, we found public places closed so we came back, invited the couple in from next door, and made our own fun. We heard people even drove to Calgary in the evening for a coffee. We did ski at Jasper a couple of weekends, but it was a long trip and we generally we skied on Edmonton's riverbank.

In the cold weather, my beard would get white with ice. Elk Island Park was always interesting because of the bison or elk roaming there. If the ice on a lake looked safe, we took our car on it and practiced spinning turns.

In the meantime, I had been looking for a job in Vancouver. When spring arrived, I flew there for a couple of days, staying with Vic and Eve while I looked for a job. My flight over the Rockies was enhanced by being allowed to sit in the cockpit behind the pilot. I got a job with Phillips Barrett Engineers (PBE), returned to Edmonton, and gave notice to my boss who said, "So you just holed up for the winter, eh?"

We were so happy to be in Vancouver, our original destination. It was March 1959. I told Heather flying over the mountains had been fabulous with their white snow cover and that Vancouver was paradise with a pleasant temperature and an interesting harbour and parks. Unfortunately, for her first five weeks, it rained continuously with dark cloud cover. Heather was very disappointed and challenged me: "How could you be so wrong?" But in the sixth week we woke to a brilliant blue sky with the local mountains gleaming white; it was like another world had returned. I had a holiday feeling when I walked to work.

Heather found a job as a legal secretary again and with the extra money we rented a one-bedroom apartment on the ninth floor where westward we could see across English Bay and eastwards, Mount Baker, 10,750' high. The apartment had a second double bed that could slide out into the living room from somewhere in the kitchen. We loved our first elevated home.

I was laid off from PBE on 24 April 1959 after six weeks because the company had not been awarded the big airport project it had bid on. I was really teed off with this decision. One of the bosses suggested that without a beard my work chances would be enhanced. I immediately shaved it off and spent a day skiing to tan my white face. They introduced me to H.A. Simons, a pulp and paper design company where I was offered a position, and I started April 27. It provided me with a year of serious work leading a team of engineers and draftsmen in producing construction drawings for a 600-foot-long major pulp and paper mill in Texas. I enjoyed every moment of the task. Using it as an example of my work, I obtained my British Columbia Professional Engineering Certification. One of the engineers who worked for me was George Forrestal, who had trained in Australia and had just arrived. We found him a place in our apartment building on Nelson Street.

During the time with Simons we made many good friends, particularly Ken Farquharson, Louis van Blankenstein, Pierre Bourquin, Graham Kelleher, George, and many others who were keen on hiking, tennis or skiing. Pierre introduced us to many of his Swiss friends while he made wonderful fondues in his apartment. We sat around the pot on the floor, leaving rather Japanese-flag-looking stains on the carpet from all the fondue droppings.

With the Simons project completed, Heather and I were just leaving on a two-week holiday when I received in Saturday's mail notice that I was going to be laid off on 29 May 1960. I was probably one of fifty laid off as that was the practice when work was completed and no other projects were available. We took our holiday and then I searched again for another job. Through my

Simons boss, I very quickly got a contact, an interview, and was accepted on 30 May 1960. My new employer was Wright Engineers Limited (WEL), an international mining consulting company of twenty-five people, recently started by Harold and Len Wright. These changes of job were fortunately very fast with no significant loss of salary.

I worked at WEL for two challenging boom years. I was involved in the development of most major mines as a civil engineer, designer and project manager. We designed and built most of the big mines in British Columbia and got used to daily pressure to meet operational deadlines and costs. The pace of work at that time was frenetic, as mines were being built by the company on a regular basis in British Columbia as well as overseas.

After a couple of small projects, my first major project was leading a team of engineers and draftsmen in the design of structural systems for a coal, potash and sulphur loadout terminal at Port Moody. It included a dock, loadout handling systems and three massive A-frame buildings for storage of the materials. This had many interesting and challenging features including the ability to handle the three materials on one system, special piling, pre-loading of soil conditions to minimize its settlement, and the A-frame buildings. To be sure of what was happening at the site, and checking progress, I often made my private inspection visits early on Saturday mornings. Once when walking down the concrete tunnel into the underground car dumper pit, I was surprised to find water had leaked into the pit and up the tunnel. After the water was pumped out, the small leak was epoxied solid.

During our working days, Heather and I managed a "let's do it" active social life, and on seeing all the wonderful boats in the water from our window, decided to learn to sail. We bought a 15′ Snipe for $200 and used to sail after work whenever possible, as it was conveniently moored on a buoy off a marina on Kitsilano Beach. We took our friends out on it many times, once turning it over and needing to be rescued. When not sailing, we hiked the local mountains or played tennis. In the winter we skied locally or we'd get picked up by friends, generally our Swiss friend, Pierre Bouquet, at 6 a.m. outside our building to go skiing at Mount Baker. It was a vibrant skiing area with so much snow that many times chains had to be put on the rear wheels so we could get up the road to the lodge. On occasions, the snowbank was 20 feet high at the side of the road. We also played tennis in the winter, having discovered three indoor wood courts tucked away at UBC. We could take friends in our car as I had passed the BC driving test, well only just, although I had already taken tests in Ontario, Quebec and Alberta. I was so relaxed about the BC test that I actually ran out of gas on Denman Street. The inspector had to get out and walk back to his office while I pushed the car to a service station. When I returned to his office his colleagues were looking rather smug, but I passed.

One wonderful day, Heather told me she was pregnant. The baby, Jeremy, was born on 17 July 1961. In those days, a new mum could spend a week or two in the Grace Hospital. Well, after a 10lb 4oz baby, you needed a rest. The doctor who shook my hand after the birth certainly looked as though he needed a rest. With his straw blond hair, Jeremy was a great hit and was carried everywhere in a box I made that conveniently fitted into a pram. Thus, if we were going out to dinner, we could carry him into the apartment without waking him — simple, really. We loved every moment with him: his smile, his tricks and his baby smell (but not all smells). After a few months, he went in my rucksack when we went skiing. At the Mt. Baker ticket centre, there used to be a picture of me lining up with Jeremy's head peeking out of the rucksack.

There was a bit of disruption in the week after Jeremy arrived. I had to go to the super rich copper Craigmont mine site at Merritt for five weeks while I helped correct the vibrations being caused by some high-powered crushing machines. Heather's method of avoiding Jeremy's high-powered newborn screams was to turn the radio up and continue reading.

When my mum retired, we paid for her to come out to see some part of *our* world. She arrived in early 1961 wearing trousers, having thought she had better get on with it. It was a good choice, as we took her up to up to Banff to see the Rockies and brought her back through the States. I did a bit of skiing out of the Temple Mountain Lodge because Heather was pregnant. One night, an elderly couple was looking for a game of bridge, and my mum and I offered our services. Without thinking, I once said to her, "Don't forget we're venereal," a phrase we often used in the army in place of "vulnerable" and she said, "Patrick," in a sharp tone. The other man said, "I don't think we heard that." We weren't asked again.

The mining industry was developing to a peak, and in the winter, I arrived in morning darkness at WEL and left in the dark. As the company grew, many members were investing in mining shares, while calling their brokers during the day to check what the market was doing. In fact, so many calls out were being made that I suggested to management they have one person checking for those involved, to save time being wasted. At lunch, many of us would cross the road and enter C.M. Oliver, mining brokers.

As we went through their doors, we would be hit by the hot, fetid breath of greed from the packed shoulder-to-shoulder crowd. On one side of the biggish room was a raised narrow walkway allowing two or three staff to keep marking in chalk the share prices as they changed. On the opposite side of the room was a line of several three- to four-foot-wide enclosures, each with a broker, so trading could be easily carried out or information obtained. It was a madhouse. During the summer a big-name-mining-speculator might blow into town to boost his 26-cent stock and by the end of summer, it might have been pushed up to 41 cents — time to sell before it dropped over winter. At one point, more stock was sold on the local market than in New York. In an interesting side note, from my WEL office I could see the ferry terminal at the bottom of Burrard Street — now gone.

There were always lessons to be learned in the investing business. Once, on the advice of a friend, I first bought silver at about $7 an oz. A short while later, I bought more at $12 an oz. only to watch it sizzle up to $48. While I was thinking about all the things I could buy, it dropped overnight, but I managed to break even. It was a lesson learned about speculation.

A second lesson came when Bre-X came on the market. I had been reading in the *Financial Post* about this gold mine development in Kalimantan, Indonesia. I called the company's office in Calgary to let them know we were doing a lot of work there with ports and coal mines and had an office in Jakarta. I also suggested their stock, now at $12, was doing well and the executive there said, "It will be $17 next week." I immediately bought shares at $14, and then more at $20. With frequent announcements from Bre-X and local brokers saying the resource had moved from 30 million oz. of gold to 70 million oz., even 200 million oz., and with stock splits, the mine was a recommended buy. One broker even gave a target of $270. It was a false frenzy.

I was in England on holiday when I called my broker to see whether my value at $170 had increased, and he told me the bad news — it had just dropped out of the sky. My stomach flipped, but then he reminded me I had put on a stop loss, saving about 90% of the value. Lucky. After the call to my broker, I drove into a quiet field and sat there pondering where the mine might be going.

I concluded investors would likely invest again as this was the first loss. So, I called my broker again and asked him to re-invest a third of the money I had made. He did so and I made a bit more before the whole deal collapsed.

Although I always invested, I never seriously thought about a pension for the future until I was in my 50s, as I reckoned it was for older people. The wrong policy. In today's climate, it seems that 40% of Canadians would be in trouble if they were to miss out on one pay cheque. Fortunately, Heather and I rarely experienced such marginal living but then house prices had not risen as they have today through foreign buying demand.

Like all good things, I was beginning to see the mining market start to slow down and we were often looking around in the office for work to do. I was surprised to see how morale, which had been so high, could drop so quickly when work did not fully occupy the office staff. I did not like the idea of sitting around waiting for the next project, so Heather and I considered where to go or what to do next.

During our time in Vancouver, we had met many Australians. We had enjoyed their company and playing tennis together and were always interested in what they told us about their country. After reviewing as much data as we could, we decided to emigrate there — a major decision.

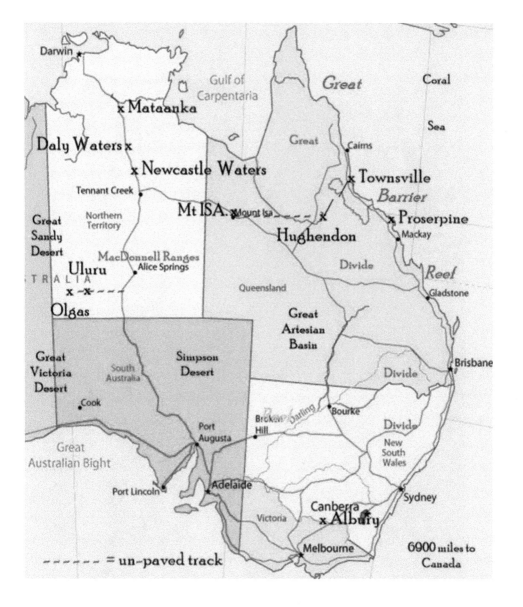

Our Trip:
Mt. Isa to Ayers Rock (Uluru) and Olgas to Darwin then Mt. Isa to
Cairns Proserpine, Barrier Reef, Brisbane, Canberra, Melbourne and
England.

Start

of

our

Outback

trip

CHAPTER 10

Outback Australia
1962–1963
Travel to Australia

I left WEL on 23 February 1962, on good terms with Harold and Len Wright and the staff, to return if I came back to Vancouver. It was a big step. Within a remarkably short time we applied to emigrate and booked a trip to Fiji on P&O's *Oriana* and would fly from there to Sydney.

The departure from the downtown dock was a throbbing scene as friends came to see us off along with other well-wishers. Many people were allowed on the ship until the hooter went, and then had to leave. Ashore, people hurled coloured ribbons to their friends from the dock and onto the ship, it was so close. It was a highly emotional moment as the ship moved away from the dockside, breaking the ribbons, unlike the controlled security departures of today. Aboard with Heather and Jeremy, who was one year old, life was very comfortable. We met up with Ozzy, an architect, and his wife Sandi, from Mercer Island, Seattle and enjoyed their company. Ozzy was one of the most inquisitive men I had ever met. We always had interesting discussions. This trip was much calmer than my freighter voyage to Canada, and for this I was truly thankful.

Fiji was hot and humid. A taxi ride through the lush green countryside took us to a tired, somewhat run-down wooden waterfront hotel. It was as if we had stepped back in time. In the lounge, heads might peek around the sides of newspapers as if checking us out, and it required a certain amount of restraint, not to say some disreputable words, to stir the place up.

In the restaurant, the waitresses sprayed insecticide under the tables from time to time so we were not too disturbed by insects. As we retired to our room at night, toads or frogs delighted us as they hopped along the corridor in front of us. It was quite a different place, but the beach waterfront was pristine, lined with rich coloured flowers. In trips around the country, young lads might climb up a palm tree, bring back a coconut, and split it open for us to sample the rich and refreshing juice. All locals, it seemed, wanted to hold Jeremy while they admired his straw blond hair. Fijians and Indians seemed to be the two groups who occupied the island.

It was here that I received a cable from my past boss, Harold Wright (he was an Olympic sprinter in 1932), asking me to divert to New Zealand to inspect and report on an old mine. I was happy to do this.

Changing our flight, we carried on to New Zealand and stayed at the Rob Roy Hotel in Waihi just south of Auckland. It had the lumpiest bed we had ever slept in, but the rich, harmonious Maori singing and laughter in the bar in the evening was a delight which we looked forward to on following evenings.

In earlier days, the gold mine had been the largest in the world, but because the process had been so inefficient, much gold had been lost in the waste tailings. With the high price of gold, and with better recovery systems, it was thought the tailings could be profitably re-worked. After working with a mining engineer there and looking at the remnants of the infrastructure for a week, I could not make a positive report. Before we left, we rented a car, which I am sure had a governor to restrict its speed and were able to visit the Rotorua hot springs and have a good tour of the countryside.

We later knew a couple who sailed into Fiji. Two days later when sailing south, they encountered a power boat which had run out of fuel and was in danger of being blown out into the ocean. Fortunately for the people aboard, our friends towed them back to Fiji. Two weeks later they had to leave Fiji as the celebratory parties for their return were too overwhelming.

Working in New South Wales

After a week, we flew on to Australia, and while I looked for work, we rented a place close to the waterfront. At night we could hear the pounding of massive waves on the coastal rocks. Later, we found a cheaper unit in Kirribilli, a short ferry ride from Circular Quay, downtown Sydney. I found the first impression of the city disappointing, as it looked remarkably like London or an English town, with its redbrick houses, red-tiled roofs, and red buses. I am not sure what I was expecting, but it was a bit of a shock and quite a change from the wooden houses in Vancouver. We were looking forward to joining up again with Australian couples we had met in Vancouver, Vic and Eve May, and later in Canberra, Graeme and Fleur Kelleher. Graeme was later to become the chairman of the Great Barrier Reef Marine Park.

Contrary to what we had expected, we found Australians rather formal compared to the freer ways of Canadians, although quite outgoing. Was this some residual characteristic from past English ways? The formality flowed through job interviews. One interviewer said rather snootily, "We don't normally hire engineers without university degrees," and the interview terminated rather abruptly when I responded, "Where is the interview going then?" Strangely enough, I found the same type of formality when later working in South Africa. It took a long time to find a job I wanted, and after three or four weeks I was getting rather desperate, especially when one government interviewer wanted to know how I would measure the height of a tree. I felt like saying I would cut it down and pace it out.

Finally, on 7 May 1962, I found a field job out of town on a site. It was with the Department of Public Works of New South Wales to look after raising the nine 270-foot spans of the Bethanga Bridge some 10 feet to accommodate more water storage in the hydroelectric Hume Weir Dam. My interview with the chief engineer and the principal engineer had been in their offices. However, when I went to get my papers a few days later, I had to go through their main office and realized I had perhaps made a mistake in job selection. Desks were piled with files tied with pink tape, and there was a whiff of bygone days. Some people wore waistcoats with watch chains, and I could swear there was cigarette ash down their fronts. I later learned that there were some senior engineers called "retreads" (like worn tyres that were re-treaded) who had retired but had come back to work at a junior's salary. This was a government department.

Prior to working at Hume Weir, I had to go to Oberon to help out on a small 4 x 7 x 3,500 ft long tunnel that was being driven through wet decomposed granite under a compressed air system. Without the compressed air, the sides and ceiling of this wet material kept failing and partly filling the tunnel.

Our newly purchased used Volkswagen carried us off the paved roads of Sydney and onto red dusty gravel tracks through bush and gum-treed terrain. The occasional wallaby would leap out of the bush and bounce alongside for a while, much to our surprise and amusement. We stopped the night at a small hotel where the guests sat at a single table for dinner and breakfast. I thought this was a warm, friendly option for hotels. Our stopover upset authorities, as my expense allowance for the journey was for only a day trip.

The government accommodation was a small wooden house with minimal old furniture. Overnight it became quite cold, there being no insulation, and Oberon being the highest village in the Snowy Mountains. Seeing the ground through cracks in the living room floor did not help, either. I chopped up wood logs inside on the floor for our fire. Another way to warm our thin blood from the soft living of Western Canada was to turn on every electrical gadget, including the hot shower in the morning, to get warm. Later, the man who read our meters asked Heather if we had any extra appliances because we were using more electricity than all the six other houses on the road. Actually, in the mornings it was warmer to sit outside in the rising sun while we listened to kookaburras with their powerful caw-caw-cawing and their manic screeching. This always meant we started the day in a good mood.

We were there some four weeks while I undertook survey work and other jobs. The progress in this small tunnel seemed slow, like 3 ft per three-shift day (three miners per shift), and 21 feet per week, so I queried the bonus system for the miners. I was told the government did not have bonus systems. Having just come from a leading mine consultant, I said I had never heard of a miner working without a bonus system. After looking at the cost figures, I argued with my boss that the contractor was set for an early retirement since he was on a cost-plus contract and his equipment was hired out at about three times the cost of the labour. So I suggested we could pay the miners a bonus to motivate increased progress and reduce the project cost. Well, with the bonus (extra money for progress over 30 ft/week) in place, the progress each day went up 50% — a great success for which I did not receive the appropriate credit, or bonus.

Finally, we were driving down to Canberra on our way to Hume (pronounced 'ume) Weir, located on the Murray River to start on the bridge project. The dam was located close to Albury, a busy sheep farming town. On the way, we stayed for the night with Graeme and Fleur, whom we had met in Vancouver, and had a fine evening catching up on their life since leaving Vancouver.

When I got out of our car at the dam site office, the minimal scope of the place was a disappointment. Worse, the following day I was to learn that the job was not to raise the bridge 10 feet but only to replace the bearings. How could the senior engineers who interviewed me be so lacking in knowledge of their own project? My concern was that I knew it was going to be difficult to obtain another job from this remote location, and I needed good experience to obtain membership in the Institution of Civil Engineers in the UK.

Although we enjoyed the warm friendship of our neighbours and their hospitality to these *pommies* (a disparaging term for a Brit immigrant) I started searching for another more challenging project. Being called a *pommie* was sometimes used disparagingly, but if addressed as a "bloody pom" it was more affectionate, and you were making progress. Some ten families lived on the road of our second supplied government house. On the second day, a neighbour came over and with a strong Aussie accent advised,

""'Ello, luv. You should cut the lawn so you can see any snakes because they are quite poisonous, and your lad should wear shoes."

Poisonous snakes and spiders were a problem, and you never put a hand in a hole without checking it out first. Walking to work across a field, I generally carried a stick to deal with snakes. Once a snake came at me up a stone embankment on the dam and I had to kill it with a rock. Heather had her own experience when she left the car to buy a couple of things in a shop. When returning, she opened the car door and a snake came out from under the car, giving her quite a shock. She asked the shopkeeper for help; he came out with an axe handle and bopped it one saying, "That should fix it!" It was a relief, for Jeremy was still in the car.

Heather and I played a lot of tennis there and were fully accepted into the friendly activities of the local club. For her first inter-club home match, our neighbour suggested Heather "bring a plate," which she did, only to find there was supposed to be something on it. Later, she took her homemade rock cakes, but then our neighbour suggested for the following week's match Heather bring the cream, and the neighbour would make a sponge cake. We were still on a learning curve! Once when we were playing on their red gravel courts, I heard this increasing metallic roar. I first thought it was something to do with the nearby rail yard, but then I realized all the players were tearing into the clubhouse. It was a deluge of large hailstones hitting the corrugated roofs, and I joined the players, dashing for shelter before being battered.

The rolling hills around us were full of wildlife and in some areas, we could follow the trenching along a fault line where, in earlier days, gold had been extracted. In the sun, the grassy undulating hills were yellow with buttercups then turned green in the rain when the petals closed. Many towns with tongue-twisting Aussie names were nearby: Wagga Wagga, Jindabyne, Yarrawonga and Wangaratta. In Albury we were most impressed to see the long rows of rich green grass tennis courts occupied by tennis hopefuls dressed in white and being coached on Saturday morning — this was the home of Margaret Court who won a Wimbledon singles title. In town, I chuckled to hear a woman telling her other half on a Saturday morning, "'Ere's ten bob. Don't spend it all in the pub and be back 'ere in an hour."

The work was not taxing, especially in contrast to the engineering magazines that I had read months earlier in Canada, but I was urgently seeking more challenging work. In the meantime, we enjoyed the new life but I found it difficult to be called Mr. Hill in the office by our next-door neighbour and then "Pat" over the fence or a beer. Once I was invited to the local ski club meeting, where we spent the whole evening discussing how to crush all the beer cans. At a sort of Lions meeting the plan was to obtain money for a local charity by hiring a truck and axes one weekend to chop trees down for firewood to be sold later. My suggestion that, because of the effort required, the high risk to our limbs, and the minimal profit, we should just stay in bed and kick in ten shillings each, was not met favourably. Sometimes, there would be a dance in the community hall where the women would have their dance shoes on with straps winding up and around their calves. They danced with gusto, and you learned to avoid their twirling legs, as tennis might be out for a week. This was indeed a different life!

At this time, it seemed everyone in Australia was trying to find a duck-billed platypus, and there were radio programs asking you to call in if you had seen one. Below the Hume Weir Dam, there was a marvellous, quiet and secluded stilling pond where we could lie on a concrete block just above the water and watch them along with turtles and a myriad of different birds.

Working in Queensland

I eventually left the Public Works department on 7 December 1962 after getting a new job on 14 December 1962 as a field engineer for construction of a new copper mine at Mt. Isa in northwest Queensland. We flew up there as soon as possible while our car went by train. This area was classed "remote" and had a double taxation allowance. This meant I would receive double the normal allowance for a wife and child, which would give us some extra money. We landed a week before Christmas 1962 in a temperature of 113°F. As we were driven to our hotel, I had to deflect the side window draft away from me, because the blast it created was too hot and stifling. That night, there was a tremendous electrical storm followed by an enormous crash as a nearby substation was hit and the lights went out. Next day, when I started work on the site in my "office," an 8 x 8 x 8-foot corrugated shed, it was 115 degrees (46.1C). A considerable amount of excavation was underway with trucks and equipment passing by all day.

As the new houses in Happy Valley ready for the major copper concentrator project were not quite finished, we were provided with a rented house. The owner, who had his own "station" [farm], wore a wide-brimmed hat, spoke slowly, and had intense blue eyes; Heather was fascinated. We were there for eight weeks and enjoyed some new experiences. The time a lizard fell off the ceiling onto our bed demonstrated a new decibel level for Heather's vocal cords and a new *Guinness Book of World Records* entry as she exploded from the bed. We experienced the buzzing sounds and red eyes at night as insects of various types tried to force their way through the wooden louvered windows; the hornet that decided to make its nest in the kitchen; the intriguing 6-to-8-inch stick insect that did push-ups on the side of a mango tree in the garden; the incredibly noisy and brilliant thunderstorms; and a horse that came into the garden to get at the mangoes. We made a plastic pool for Jeremy who spent the time leaping in and out and splashing around.

"Isa" [Mt. Isa] received only about 10–12 inches of rain a year which fell in two months; the rest of the year was dry. If the clouds travelled down the catchment areas, the rain would fall in the run-off. This it did while we were there and caused the Leichhardt River (which split the town from the mine) to rise eight feet in an hour or two from a mere ten-foot-wide trickle and spread two hundred yards across the low-lying ford. At this point, the entertainment started as cars still tried to cross the low-level concrete road. Going too fast they'd flood and stall, only to be followed by trucks that tried to push them across. Meantime, people who had anything that would float would leap into the river upstream and shoot through this main crossing to the cheers of the onlookers, many of whom were customers of the strategically located Argent Hotel overlooking the river. School children gleefully looked at teachers stuck on the other side of the floodwater, which lasted about three hours before it went down as fast as it had risen.

I was working for a joint Australian-American venture, and the project was to build a new copper concentrator plant. There seemed to be a bit of a pro-American bias in the air, and I put this down to Australians trying to break free from the ubiquitous British influence. Part of my job was to survey and monitor the removal of all the old tailings and build up the ground some 80' with solid fill. At 7 a.m., I would prop up one side of my corrugated iron shack and work there in tremendous heat and dust with earth-moving trucks and equipment passing all the time. It was a grubby job with red dust over everything. I wore elastic-sided boots to keep the dust out, shorts and a T-shirt. Within thirty minutes, I was soaked, and had to re-charge with water from my porous water bag hanging in the shade. A cooling breeze was a mixed blessing as it just created more dust. At one time, the removal of the vertical wall of the tailings collapsed in an avalanche and those in the pit had to run for safety. After that, the height was reduced using a small dozer on a cable held by a big dozer, lowered down to reduce the face height of the pit — a good idea but it needed care. Every month I had to agree with the client the quantities moved. I had a young Texan lad to help with the survey, and Heather was always impressed at being addressed as "ma'am."

Soon we moved into our new company house built in Happy Valley with all new furniture. It was a very pleasant moment, especially being our first new house. We built a chicken-wire fence corral in the shade to keep Jeremy from wandering out of the yard, but he soon learned that he could repeatedly fall against it and knock it low enough so he could escape and we would have to search the neighbourhood for him. The house was built on three-foot concrete stilts with a metal barrier on the top to keep the wood-eating *teredos* out. Sometimes we had to lure Jeremy out from underneath the house with tempting bananas before he encountered any poisonous insect. I did not wish to search for him under the house.

At the weekend, we enjoyed exploring the wild countryside. Once we drove along a riverbed to a pool to swim there with friends; some of the rock walls around had paintings on them by Aboriginals. On less strenuous days, we spent our time trying to cool off at the local Lake Moondarra, which was just being formed. Shade was at a premium since the sun was very hot and the sky an intense blue. Jeremy was a wanderer and could be a devil to find. At the local public pool, he was finally found jumping on the manager's bed. At the same pool, Heather was asked to leave because the manager thought her bikini was too skimpy. In Vancouver, we had always used Bikini Beach, close to the entrance to Stanley Park, where bikinis were more acceptable than on the main beaches.

The mine showed films on an outside screen in the evenings while we managed to join up with some local lads to play tennis under floodlights. No matter how long we played with them, they would always address Heather as "Mrs. Hill." Did we look that old? Each night there seemed to be a different kind of insect ranging from a solid, heavy-duty winged maybug, which could be swatted to the other end of the court, or some type of large-winged moth. One super player was an Indonesian student living in Australia on the Colombo Plan. He admired our Canadian First Nations carvings and said we must come and see his. This did not occur, but when we all went to see him fly off home from the one-shack airport, we returned to our car only to find all his carvings on the front seat. We were overwhelmed by this gesture, but sadly were never able to locate him again.

After a while, the second-in-command for the project arrived from the States. He didn't shake hands with any of us in the office and quickly started to find fault with all that we did. He and I soon did not see eye to eye, and he started to make life a real chore. I would return home so fired up that I grabbed anything to read to distract my mind, so I could get a 15-minute "kip" to release the tension. When, unbelievably, he removed my site transport, leaving me to walk everywhere, this was the limit. When no one picked me up to take me back for lunch, I took a cab home and back, and gave the bill to the accountant. This caused a ruckus, which caused my departure in August 1963. The project manager, with whom I had a good relationship, explained there was nothing he could do. Five weeks later, I heard the unpopular man was sent back to the States; I suspect he had some serious problems. It was fortunate I had already worked the eight months required to obtain the lower tax rating. One office secretary cried when I said goodbye; perhaps being a local, she was not used to the harder ways of life.

Touring to Ayers Rock, Darwin, Barrier Reef and Canberra

By this time, we were on a six-week trip to cross the Northern Territory to Alice Springs, Ayers Rock, and the Olgas in the Gibson Desert, then north to Darwin, east to Cairns and Cooktown and finally down the coast to Canberra. We were thrilled to be free and roaming the unknown before I returned to the UK for further study.

Living in the Australian Outback was a fascinating experience with its remoteness, rich and changing colours, wildlife, insect life, and lack of people. We drove along in our old Volkswagen, which we had equipped with spare oil and gas tanks, tyres, homemade roof rack, shovel, and our porous water bag on the front bumper. I even built a chicken-wire frame to protect the front window from stones kicked up by passing cars; this had happened once before, giving me a shock to see my whole window glaze over with cracks and then collapse on me. Before night fell, we pulled off the road or rather track to a secluded spot, kicked some gum tree twigs and leaves together and, in a flash, had a fire to billy-up on. We also had a mini stove that worked on gasoline I could obtain by lowering a small tin down into the Volkswagen gas tank. As Heather prepared our supper, I pumped up our two *lilos* – inflatable air mattresses that were a wedding present from Peter Lawrence, one of the few English students with whom I studied – and prepared for a night sleeping out in the open; we never used a tent and always put Jeremy in the back of the car.

The evening was a time when we could totally relax; well, you could do no more until the morning, especially as we had no light except a flashlight. Once Jeremy was down, we could just lie back and absorb nature. There were only a few mosquitos, and we rarely thought of snakes, spiders or ants, even though some of the latter were over an inch long.

We were enraptured by the utter blackness contrasting with the brilliance of the stars, the likes of which we had not seen before in such clear and unpolluted air. There was nobody else for miles around and no sound. In the amphitheatre of the Milky Way, planets and galaxies hung low over us, and it was sometimes so bright it was almost possible to read. We would watch the orb of lights slowly revolve accompanied by the occasional streak of a falling star or meteorite. We could see satellites clearly as they orbited the planet. Each night was an incredible experience only enhanced by the soothing draw on our cigarettes. Soon, drowsiness would come as we buried our heads under a sheet and cruised until dawn.

We were reminded of the joke when Sherlock Holmes and Dr. Watson were camping in the Outback. Holmes woke Watson and asked him what he deduced from the myriad stars and planets overhead. Once awake, and after a moment's thought, Watson observed that because there were so many, there must be a planet similar to earth, and therefore people like us. To this, Holmes said, "No, no, you bloody fool! Someone has swiped our tent!"

We were usually woken by the calls and chattering of birds, Jeremy calling out for "hot tea," or the first rays of the sun clearing the distant flat horizon. We ate fairly quickly as we made our sandwiches for the day. There was a good reason for this as we found that when the *mossies* disappeared in the morning, there was only about half an hour before we were engulfed by a million flies. They stuck on anything damp – our eyes, back or head – and because they might have been feasting on dead cattle, we put a smear of Vaseline around Jeremy's eyes to minimize any chance of infection. We had to get moving to avoid them, which we did by driving off. With the windows open, we whirled a towel around a few times, which reduced the number in the car to about 500. At night, there was another half hour of peace when the flies disappeared and before the *mossies* arrived. This was certainly a very different climate from Vancouver. I can't emphasize enough the number of flies, especially near water or damp areas, and the way they were constantly irritating. When entering a house, we would always knock the flies off the back of the person entering before us and passing the fly screen. Once when Jeremy was screaming, we found him standing on an ant's nest with minute green ants working their way up his legs, biting him. Not pleasant.

Early one morning we had just woken up when we heard the roar of big trucks, and as two tore past, their drivers waved at us. We thought one of them might be the father of a couple of Aussies, Tim and Fay, that we had met in Vancouver. We'd heard their dad had a trucking company. We finished our breakfast and caught up with them about two hours later in the middle of nowhere when they were having their breakfast. The father, Fred, was crouched over the fire, eating a sausage, when I walked up and said, "'Ow yer goin', Mr. Drewes?" He stopped with the sausage halfway to his mouth, looked rather perplexed, and said, "I know you from somewhere!" We stopped for a cuppa, told him where we were going and that we hoped to see him back in Sydney. While we chatted, one of the drivers kept waving the flies off Jeremy saying, "Get away, yer black sods, get away, yer black sods…"

Alice was a small community and a fair was on. There were many Aboriginals or "Abos." We stopped only one night, which was long enough for a quick look and to collect some more supplies together with a couple of copies of the famous painter, Namitjira's brilliantly coloured Aboriginal paintings.

Unfortunately, we were not there at the time of the "British" Henley-on-the-Todd boat race. This is a mad race where "eights" are boat-looking frames with a crew of eight standing inside the frame and holding it up, racing down the dry sandy stream bed of the Todd River. Crazy, yes, but it was a big event.

Just out of Alice and on our way to Ayers Rock on a rough track, there was a small sign partially hidden behind a bush saying, "To Ayers Rock, next gas stop, Kulgerra, 188 miles." Fortunately, we saw it in time and got on the right track. A driver that had missed the sign caught up with us a few days later having gone a full day southward towards Adelaide before realizing his mistake. The first night out from Alice, said to be the Centre of the Red Zone, we pulled off the track, started our fire, and settled down for the night. Later, as we heard the engine of a truck, we also heard drunken voices shouting out "Yer 'on a bloody private paddock!" Amazing they would complain as there was nothing around us, but perhaps they were somewhat hungover from the Alice show.

Our rough track passed through Henbow, Erldunda, and Curtin Springs, and between were semi-arid lands with scrub, spinifex, and gum trees. The dust was brilliant red and infiltrated everywhere. We put a tampon over our carburetor to keep the dust out. We had to watch out for "bull dust," which was just like flour and could be white. It concealed holes in the track, gave no support to the car and provided a nasty unexpected bump and shock if you hit a pothole too fast.

The key rule if your car bogged down in the loose soil or sand was not to try and rev your way out but to get out, thoroughly inspect the problem, and decide how to get out prior to digging in deeper. There were very few cars; we might see two or three a day.

One morning when we were some way off the track for the night, the engine did not want to start, which was one hell of a shock. No digging would get us to the track where we could try to push-start it, and there was no way to push it in the soft soil. While I was swearing and cursing in near panic that a car might not come through for a day or more, messages flitted into my head with what, I thought and hoped, was a flash of brilliance. We would boil up some water and pour it into and over the battery with the possibility of getting some ions flowing. This we did, worked our worry beads, prayed for ten minutes, and with the tension building, turned on the ignition. We yelled with relief as it started and we danced around, hugging each other as it roared away. This was in the middle of nowhere. Were we going bonkers?

The massive monolith of Ayers Rock (2,820 ft altitude) grew impressive as it loomed on the flat plain. It is so flat that in its 1,000 square miles, no watercourse exists. Uluru, the rock's Aboriginal name, rises over 1,400 ft from the plain and is 2½ miles long and ½ mile wide. This ancient hallowed ground of the Aboriginals was first discovered by a European in 1873. As we drew closer, immense striations and channels appeared to be running from one side and over the top to the other side.

We drove around looking for a way up. There were none but at one point, I tried to drive the VW up its sloping rock side as far as I could while Heather waited with Jeremy. It was not a bad try, but we'd probably be locked up if I tried that now. There were only four or five cars there that evening as we drank our tea and watched from afar the slow magical transition of the brilliant red mass to a delicate purple-blue and then finally to a dark mass as the sun dropped below the horizon. Today, there are paved roads, hotels and camping resorts, an airport and a university, with over a quarter of a million visitors a year. Perhaps it is no wonder that climbing up the rock is no longer allowed. We were fortunate to be there in the early days.

The following day we drove around the rock, overwhelmed by the magnitude of the striations and near-vertical rock face. Looking into caves at the bottom, we searched for Aboriginal paintings. This is sacred territory for the Aboriginals; surprisingly, it might be called Dreamtime country as the massive monolith is such a landmark. There are apparently more than twenty myths associated with the caves, wall faces, and other parts of Uluru. A fascinating glimpse of the Aboriginal culture can be experienced in the translated names such as *Jinindi Rockhole*, made by willy-wagtail women; *Ijari-Jari*, wet-weather camp of the marsupial mole; and *Holes in Rock Face*, made by spears thrown by poisonous snakes. There is a story where the *Kangaroo Rat Hero* let his tail slope way down to ground level at a point called *Webo* so that the traveller could make his ascent of the Rock.

After our exploration in virtual solitude around the rock's perimeter caves, we climbed it from *Webo*. The average temperature was 30°C/86°F; the peak record was 47°C/116°F — pretty much the same as my Isa site working temperature.

In 1963, there was no handrail, and the openness of the rock slope made you climb carefully and be thankful there was no wind blowing. There were stories that some thirty people have fallen off in recent years down the steep 1,000 ft sides. Heather and I started up optimistically with Jeremy in my rucksack, but I decided against that, turned back and left him with Heather. With my Achilles tendons stretched to the limit, I finally made it to the upper level. At the top, it was like being at sea with an unlimited flat horizon all around and an immense, intense blue sky above. The countryside looked pretty bleak, except for the outstanding view of the Olgas 25 miles away. Through the clear dry atmosphere, I could see Mt. Harris 100 miles away. To my surprise, there was a small tree at the top and nearby a small pool with a minute turtle in it. How did it get there?

After I'd had my fill of the unlimited 360-degree views I started down the rock face which seemed to fall away all too quickly. Our VW Beetle below looked diminutive. I was relieved I did not have Jeremy. Carefully descending down the scaly rock surface, I found my toes tried to force themselves through the front of my shoes. Later a chain was installed for visitors to hold onto, and there was a continuous line of sightseers heading for the summit. Heather then climbed to the top and when she returned said she had a weird feeling that she never wanted to come down. Perhaps this was the spiritual spell of Australia's centre or because she was up there on her own.

Once down, we drove over the rough track through the scrub

bush, gum trees and spinifex out to the Olgas. This enormous pile of granite rocks, the highest over 600 ft higher than Uluru, was equally fascinating. It looked like a collection of huge brown Hovis loaves cut up and thrown indiscriminately around with gum trees, gullies and crevasses between. It is said by Aboriginals that the carvings there were not done by humans.

We explored for a day and then headed back to Alice. Near to town we stopped at a "station" to ask for gas as we were running low. The owners were away, but the Aboriginal farmhands and families all came out to see us. They were overcome by Jeremy's straw blond hair and could not resist picking him up and passing him around. When we opened the hood, they saw his potty and realized what the splash guard (in the form of a dog's head) was for. They all went into hysterics and were doubled up with laughter — so much for our western culture. The senior patriarch drew himself up proudly for a close-up photo, complete with the usual fly or two on his face.

We then headed up the "strip," a narrow 10-foot-wide black-topped road built by the Americans during the war, to Darwin, passing through Banka Banka, Newcastle Waters, Daly Waters, Mataranka and Annaburboo. At the sight of the first car coming towards us, I ill-advisedly hogged the blacktop to avoid going in the rough, but the other car threw up so many stones I was thankful I had built a chicken-wire frame across our windscreen to stop it from being broken. With subsequent cars, I got off the blacktop when passing. When a truck "train" pulling three trailers came weaving down the road towards us, we got well out of the way. In most places we travelled, there was little traffic and if we stopped for any reason, the next car, if there was one, would usually slow down to see if we were "Okay, mate?" Everyone is conscious that being stopped in the Outback indicated a problem.

In some remote places if a car does break down, it is suggested that you stay with your vehicle, in the shade if possible, as people have been known to die of dehydration trying to walk for help. If you become desperate, it is possible to drink the water from the car radiator. Anti-freeze is not used.

The country always surprised us by its shape and form and especially wildlife with wild camels that originally came from India to transport goods, wild horses or brumbies, snakes, wallabies, goannas (one had a body as big as my upper leg), and birds of all sorts including parrots, cockatoos, and galahs, pink and grey parrots. The galah was a stupid bird that often flew into our sloping windscreen, only to be deflected up into the air and fall down dead on the road behind. Once we had the tremendous thrill of having a wedgetail eagle with an 8-to-10-foot wingspan fly alongside the car for about 100 yards. They are the largest bird of prey in Australia and can attack snakes, rabbits, kangaroos and generally anything that moves. Having once been attacked by an owl, I certainly did not want to come face to face with this eagle. Another time when at speed, we glimpsed a small animal in the road. On backing up, we found it was a small thorny lizard about 8 inches long — the closest thing to St. George's dragon you could imagine. We were pleased we never saw any crocodiles and heard many had been killed. The deadly toxic cane toad, introduced in 1935 to kill cane beetles in Queensland, had not yet expanded across the country.

Cockatoos are normally white with a yellow crest and often kept as pets. In Mt. Isa, our American friend, whose neighbour had one, was always threatening to climb over the fence and strangle it, as it made such a noise. Parrots were most entertaining because there were so many and they had such a variety of brilliant colours. When they flew overhead in flocks and changed direction, there could be a flash of reds and greens of their underbodies and then, as they banked, the colours turned to yellows and greys. Fascinating displays.

We were still camping out each night by driving off the road or track to a secluded spot in the trees or behind a rise of land. It never rained and we never put our tent up. Most nights, we experienced spectacular apricot skies as the sun went down. We lay back in our sleeping bags, enjoyed the nightly display of falling stars and wondered again at the clarity and size of the heavens. We appreciated the need for the speed of light to measure the size of the universe knowing in one second it could go around our planet 7.5 times.

The morning sun was always welcome as its rays reached across the land and the trees were outlined in swathes of greens and yellows. We realized the colours all around us were strong but we never realized their harsh intensity until we received our slides back later in the trip; there were some remarkable colours among them. We had always thought that the colours in Namatjira's paintings were too strong, but we were to learn otherwise.

We passed by the Devil's Marbles, a small pile of granite rocks, and then went on to Daly Waters, a sleepy place with one store, a pub and a few houses all with corrugated iron roofs. We had to order a new tyre here, which was being sent up on "tomorrow's truck." We pulled over to the bush on the other side of the road and prepared to camp for the evening. Next day when the truck arrived, I went over to the store only to be told they had forgotten to load it. As we spent a second night there, our whole living process was slowing down — reading, playing cards and playing with Jeremy. The following day, the tyre arrived, as did Paul Henderson, a large Canadian hitchhiker from BC. He was on a walkabout and had been in Tasmania. He travelled with us for three days. He could play chess, luckily, and in the evening under the moonlight we could see the pieces on my small set. He always insisted there was nothing poisonous about the spiders but one night when one about the size of my hand scuttled by in the firelight, he knocked me aside as I was about to kill it, saying, "That could be dangerous."

In Darwin, a small town just recovering from a hurricane, houses were built on high concrete stilts allowing for a car, washer/dryer and other household paraphernalia to be stored in the shade while the upper part of the house with its louvered windows caught the maximum breeze. The streets were pleasantly laid out. In the post office, a certain gentleman was able to advise anybody in a very informal way where various people were or had gone to on a walkabout. We met some people in our two-day stay and were invited by one couple to see their house in the bush. Driving down a rough track, we arrived at their abode, which consisted of a concrete slab surrounded by mosquito netting within which were placed all their household effects. So you could sit there dining or having a beer, with no interference from mossies or flies, more or less.

Soon we were on the way south again to Mt. Isa. One day when it was very hot, we stopped at a billabong [pond] for a quick dip. As Heather led the way down the muddy bank and into the inviting water, I remarked that with the trees hanging down at the edges it looked like crocodile country, although at that time most had been shot out. When she was up to her waist, I took the unfair liberty of grabbing her calf. Well, I have never seen such an extraordinary reaction as she burst out of the water and surged up the mud bank. Not so strange was the polite silence the next day and the need to get my own food.

Returning via Mt. Isa, we collected the last of our chattels, said our final farewells and headed for the coast. There was only a rough track again most of the way, since the rail company had lobbied the government not to build a road but keep the delivery of copper ore via the rail. On many occasions, we had to ford rivers or open and close gates when crossing private paddocks. We passed the occasional station, with its little group of buildings with corrugated iron roofs and the usual wind-powered propeller to pump water from an artesian water source to an overhead tank. I wondered what life would be like living in such remoteness.

We slowly headed up to the Atherton Tablelands where it was cold enough that the cattle were covered in sack coats. One night while camping, we had our tent tarp over us for extra warmth and were woken by mice scurrying over us, perhaps seeking some extra warmth too. By now, we had travelled some 4,000 miles and had been camping for over a month. It was quite a tiring process driving over so many rough roads, but our Beetle did its job very well. More particularly, in all that heat and dust, Heather always managed to produce meals to keep us going — a real challenge with no fridge.

Closer to the coast and civilization, we encountered forests of lush trees and vines, interspersed with sugar cane plantations. Prior to cutting, the fields were set alight with spectacular fires to drive out all the snakes and spiders and to make it easier to harvest. There had been an ill-advised plan in the 1930s to bring in toads from overseas, mainly South America, to eat the cane beetle pest but it was a failure because the toads could not climb up the cane. Unfortunately, they proved to be prolific. They multiplied in the millions and began occupying vast areas of Australia. Dead or alive, they were toxic and were killing off most indigenous insect and animal life, including crocodiles.

Finally, we looked down onto Townsville and the vivid blues and greens of the Coral Sea and the Great Barrier Reef while Heather and I high-fived. We took a trip out to Green Island. We were entranced by the palm trees, warm sea and the absence of dust and flies. Beaches with massive stretches of yellow sand all looked splendid, but various Aussie "nasties" could make life quite unpleasant, assuming you survived their attentions. There were sharks, if you cared for an early morning or evening swim, Portuguese man-of-war stingers that could raise a fair weal or paralyze you if there were enough of them and then, thinking you had survived, you could come ashore and step on a stonefish in the sand that would shoot its barb into your foot with some very painful, if not fatal, results. They are the most venomous fish in the world. Of course, the usual dangerous and venomous Down's tiger snakes, insects and poisonous spiders were always around.

We made enquiries at Proserpine, just south of Townsville, about a trip out to see the Barrier Reef. At a local grocery store, we purchased seats in a small boat for a visit the next day. We had no idea what the reef would look like and believing the boat might visit the same part of the reef each day, I asked if the area was scoured out. The shop owner replied, "Scoured out, mate? The bloody thing's 1,000 miles long." Our travels had left us somewhat grubby and that, along with a week's facial growth, caused two ladies sitting opposite us in the boat to remark loudly, "It looks like 'e's just got out of bed," to which I replied, "You're absolutely right."

After two hours at sea, we were told we had arrived, but the wide expanse of the sea looked bare of any reef except for an occasional piece of coral sticking up above the water. We all disembarked onto a level area of coral covered with about 6–12 inches of water. At the edge, the coral dropped vertically into a deep mysterious blackness. Once on "land", we were thrilled with the myriad colours and shapes of the coral and shells and the swift flashing movements of multi-coloured fish. On the way out, we had been warned not to touch certain cone-shaped shells as a highly poisonous barb might lash out from the pointy end and, if you were struck, could bring you to a nasty paralytic end in two hours.

As we headed south, we no longer had to cross riverbeds and rough tracks and keep stopping to open up private paddock gates but drove through the highly developed Surfer's Paradise on the Gold Coast. Unfortunately, we missed the meter maids who were introduced on the streets a year later. Their alleged task was to put money into the parking meters, so users did not receive a one-pound fine. It was part of a massive promotional scheme as the maids were dressed in gold lamé bikinis and wore a typical bush hat, a sight for sore eyes, but I wondered how many traffic accidents occurred because of distracted drivers. It was quite a change from Mt. Isa where Heather had been asked to leave a public pool as her skimpy bikini was not approved.

Our fantastic trip ended in Canberra with our friends Graeme and Fleur. We'd been fortunate to have seen and experienced more of Australia than many Aussies. Reality set in with the two weeks of preparation to depart for the UK. Graeme kindly said he would sell our car for us and on a cold morning, we left Canberra by train with the Kellehers waving goodbye. It was a sad moment, and although we had enjoyed the wildness and friendly Australians, we were looking forward to our time in England before returning to Canada.

CHAPTER 11

Sailing Back to England
1963–1965

Our ship to England, the SS *Strathmore*, was on its last trip before hitting the scrapyard. In Melbourne, our friends Louis and Barbara, their family, and Heather's uncle who had earlier immigrated with his family were on the dock to see us off. There was a great cheer from them when we shouted out that the small bolt Jeremy had found and swallowed in a shop the day before had finally appeared in his last discharge. It was another emotional moment as the ship started moving with a band playing and the streamers tearing apart and sinking to the ground. There were final farewell waves and diminishing music as we headed out into the harbour.

We rolled our way across the Great Australian Bight, stopping for one night in Freemantle. Our total trip time was five weeks, much of which was across the Indian Ocean up to Colombo. This leg was very hot and humid and caused one or two fights between passengers and even between crew and passengers. A number of passengers were immigrants that had come to Australia on a subsidized ten-pound trip from England but had not liked what they experienced and were returning home; home, of course, was a familiar environment with their friends and family support. The ocean portion of the trip was quite uninteresting, and when we passed an island, I was sure the ship listed as passengers rushed to one side taking pictures.

One time, our Indian cabin steward indicated he was getting very lonely for his wife, "*Very lonely, Madam,*" and Heather had to shoo him away as he moved to get into her bunk. During the evening dances, couples had to step quickly when the ship did a bigger roll than usual. One day, the crew had organized a country fair, which included the usual fair stands, but, because this was the last trip, passengers were allowed to smash up all the ship's pottery and china — a very popular moment. At the end of the day, Heather and I were on the upper deck looking at the romantic reflections of the moon on the sea; on the deck below a crew member was encouraging a rather elderly lady to ""'Ave a go" at kicking a football through a circular hole in a wall some feet away. As the ship was rolling, she had to kick when he gave the word. Well, it went right through. When she did it again on the third shot, we went off for a drink.

In Colombo and Bombay, we were lightered ashore in lifeboats and explored the cities on foot. On each occasion, we were overwhelmed by the persistence of street peddlers, the number of people, the dirt, and the obvious poverty. In one town, we carried fresh water in a bottle that still had a gin label on it, which just showed out of my rucksack. A very persistent gentleman kept following us saying, "I buy your gin, I buy your gin," while I kept saying, "It's fresh water." After several blocks of this continued harassment, I stopped, as did my patience. I bent over, shouting at the top of my voice and right into his ear, "Fuck off," which seemed to do the trick.

A more amusing incident was watching a snake charmer on the pavement as a tourist bus stopped alongside him so he could do his show. On the first blowing of his flute, there was no reaction from within his woven basket, so he gave it a slap, in fact several slaps. Eventually, a weary-looking cobra came into view over the rim, probably looking at the tenth bus that day, and then dropped back into the basket. Finally, to complete the show, the snake charmer had to put his hand in the basket and lift the spectacled cobra up in full view for the tourists to photograph while he played his flute. Snake charming was banned in 1991.

Getting back into a lifeboat was always a dangerous moment, especially having Jeremy, as there was a lot of pushing and shoving at the dock and at the ship. Being the ship's last voyage, its departure from each harbour was always accompanied by hooters and sirens from all ships around the harbour — a special tradition recognizing the final run of a ship and rather a sad-sounding moment.

There was a kindergarten area for children, part of which was outside on the deck. Before leaving Jeremy there, I carefully inspected the whole perimeter to make sure there was absolutely no way he could escape. Often, when either of us took him there, and the steward produced a plate of goodies for the kids, there would be a wild rush and fight to take them — Jeremy did not make out well on these occasions.

Unfortunately, on this leg we had a serious outbreak of measles among the children, including Jeremy. The hospital was overfilled, and cots had to be placed in one of the dining rooms. We maintained a 24-hour watch on him and regularly had to force water into him to prevent dehydration. It was always a big fight holding his mouth open as he was only two years old. We did not believe the fierce air conditioning helped in any way, even with adults. He was in a bad way, and we carefully tended to his needs at all hours through the last part of the journey. We took turns going ashore, while one of us stayed on the ship with him.

Aden, at the bottom end of the Red Sea, seemed to be the bargain centre of the trip. Neither of us went ashore, but we saw many passengers returning loaded with packages of cheap cameras, radios and almost every kind of electronic gear.

A far more interesting visit was taking a tour bus from Suez, the bottom end of the Suez Canal, to Port Said where I picked up the ship again. Driving along the road beside the canal was like a 1,000-year transition into the past as I saw scenes that had probably not changed for years — old farms and villages interspersed with fields being watered by shadufs, which lifted containers of water from wells by an efficient counter-weighted arm; ancient Archimedes water wheels with a screw system, which were turned, lifting water up into irrigation channels; women carrying water pots on their heads; men riding donkeys with their feet just clearing the ground; small compounds at the edges of villages for men to gather; and people praying to Mecca. It was a marvellous perspective into another way of life. I was lucky to get glimpses of these ancient sights as our tour organizers were more interested in ensuring we had tea and meals in major western hotels, which did not interest me.

At the massive symmetrical pyramids, it was difficult standing before them in the heat of the day to conceive why they were built, why they were the precise shape they were, and the organization, control, and number of people required to build them. Later, I learned their spacing apparently indicated the position of certain stars 11,000 years earlier. We climbed through narrow tunnels inside to reach old rooms used to house religious symbols. There was always a musty smell sometimes displaced by a whiff of a tourist's scent — probably purchased in Aden. Outside, I took a ride on a camel, which launched into a gallop; when I look back at the picture taken, I am staggered because I was wearing my lightweight suit and, believe it or not, a tie! Where had this formality come from?

A special treat was the visit to the Cairo Museum and being allowed in to see the Tutankhamen exhibit located in a small room probably 25 x 25 feet with guards at the door and inside. Looking at the face of the sarcophagus of Tutankhamen, just three feet away inside a glass cabinet, was indeed quite spooky. With my camera resting on the glass, my picture was even spookier as his eyes seemed to penetrate the very depths of my soul.

At Athens, Heather went ashore and was thrilled with her choice, walking around the famous Acropolis Parthenon. Later, she went ashore at Marseille and Gibraltar where she climbed the rock. Jeremy was on the mend but still looked very skinny after his illness. We were most relieved when his natural laugh and liveliness returned but his grandparents, Helen and Chris, Heather's parents, must have been shocked seeing his skinny frame after disembarking at Tilbury Dock in August 1963. It was wonderful to see them. There were many hugs and kisses before we made it to the car and headed to their home in Mitcham. We were going to stay with them while I studied.

CHAPTER 12

Post-Grad Study in London
1963–64

My earlier thoughts about earning money and possibly returning to live in England had faded as we both felt we wanted to live in Canada. Australia had been interesting with its colour and wildness, but we preferred the sheltered west coast and mountains of British Columbia, particularly as its location was much closer to the UK.

While in Australia, I had planned to take a post-graduate course in either project management at Manchester University or a soil mechanics diploma course (DIC) at Imperial College in London. I had obtained grants to attend either and decided to take the latter course, which would give me the equivalent of a master's level of education to back up my current interest in design. It would allow us to live with Heather's parents in Surrey and give them the opportunity to enjoy Jeremy before we returned to Canada. We would also be close to my mum, living in Norbury, where she had moved while I was in the army.

Within a couple of weeks of starting the course in September 1963, I began to realize this subject was something unto itself and while it was interesting and useful, to make full use of it would mean a major change in the emphasis of my engineering interests. This was a disappointment at the time, and I was later to regret that I had not taken the management course, which would have blended well with the direction I was to pursue.

The course was presented by top soil specialists but they had some irksome characteristics. One professor always wrote his notes on the board; the trouble was, he stood in front of them making it difficult to read and take notes, especially when trying to listen and follow what he was expounding upon. When explaining the problem to him later and requesting a copy of his notes prior to the lecture so they could be studied beforehand, I was advised, "That is the way I have always done it." Another professor would look in the door at the start of his lecture and advise it was off that day. On the second occasion, I was after him like a shot to advise him that I had taken a year off for this course, his was the only lecture of the day for me, and I had just travelled an hour into London for it. It did no good, and I did not want to protest too much as I wanted to pass the course.

The course was difficult. My thesis was about settlement of major oil tanks, and it took a lot of time and energy. It was a great feeling of relief in 1964, after a lot of hard work, to be told I had passed and would receive a DIC.

Heather had a harder time, having lived until then with complete freedom of action. Now the delicate business of living close to her parents did not allow that kind of freedom, which for her was frustrating. Not only that, but it reminded us that with family around, there were always obligations, unlike when we only had friends. With friends, you could say, "Could we make that another night or another day?" without any offence. We were, of course, thankful for all the marvellous support from her parents and their friends. I did double glaze all the lower windows in the house, which helped to preserve heat.

At this time, I was happy, in fact exultant, to receive in the post on a Saturday morning, while in bed, a letter advising that I had been made a member of the Institution of Civil Engineers. There was a lot of whooping from me and many hugs from Heather. So many, in fact, that Helen wanted to know what was going on. There had been an examination where I was questioned by two senior engineers on my diary covering a minimum of three years' work. This was followed in the afternoon with a requirement to write an essay in three hours on one of two questions they would put to candidates on their past work.

I had been worried about whether I had passed as my friend Ken Farquharson, who had taken the test earlier, said, "If you get through the oral questioning in 20 minutes, you'll be okay." Well, my oral test, by two engineers, was 40 minutes long as I was questioned in detail on the tunnel work under compressed air that I had worked on in Australia and some earlier piling work. I thought I had probably failed, and as I walked along the bank of the River Thames during lunch, I had a thundering headache and some very depressing thoughts while trying to think positively.

In the afternoon, the essay session worsened my condition, as one of the two questions was on a subject I had never worked on, and the other was so ambiguously worded I had doubts about what angle they wanted. With others around me going forward for their second pad of paper while I was still struggling on my first page, I finally wrote that one question did not refer to work I had done and the other was ambiguous, but I was assuming what they wanted. I felt much better with this decision and got cracking. Until the letter about passing arrived, I was pretty moody.

With these two successes under my belt by mid-1964, Heather, Jeremy and I took off for France in a Bedford van that I had been converting for a camping trip. We were trying to pack in another "do it now" trip to Europe before we headed back to Vancouver. This was such a convenient way to travel, especially as I had made a special seat for Jeremy between us. The last days before departure were so hectic with completing my study thesis report and getting ready to go, I remember leaving the ferry in France with a thunderous migraine headache, driving up the nearest quiet track into a field, and collapsing onto a bunk for a long, solid sleep. I was woken softly by Heather in the morning with a cup of tea and felt so relaxed that I had no challenges for a while, just a full family life.

We toured to Zurich, meeting up with Pierre Bourquin who had returned from Canada with his wife, Unity. I had been his best man before they left. We drove on to St. Tropez, Cannes, Monaco, Nice, Menton, Ventimiglia, and down to Venice. With its waterways and wonderful buildings, it is always a delight to go exploring there. Jeremy loved his time on the beach and with all the pigeons in the main square. We returned directly north via

Langarone, the site of the massive slide disaster at the Vajont Dam, just built in 1959. As a lesson, I wanted to see the site of this disaster. In 1963, the action of filling the dam caused part of the mountain above to slide into the filling dam. The displaced water caused a wave to pass 600 feet over the top of the 800-foot-high arch dam, the biggest in the world. It swept up and down the valley opposite, damaging many villages and wiping out Langarone downstream, killing 2,000 people. The dam was not used afterwards.

Shortly after we returned to Heather's house from this relaxing holiday, we received a call from George Forrestal who had worked with me at WEL in Vancouver. He had proposed to Ursula, an English girl. He asked me, "Will you be my best man?" "Yes, of course." "Can I bring her over tomorrow?" "Yes, of course." Next day there was a knock at the door and in he burst, in a very excited state, telling us about his trip back to Poland and how beautiful all the girls were. We said, "Great, but where is Ursula?" "She's sitting in the car." So, I went out and said, "You must be Ursula. Congratulations, come on in." A week later, they were married and returned to Vancouver.

Prior to leaving England there were several farewell parties with both parents and friends present, and then it was go time. After we had our trunks and tea chests shipped to Vancouver, we said our final goodbyes to Heather's parents and my mum and family — an unhappy moment again, but I was now looking forward to getting back to work, buying a house, and starting our own home.

CHAPTER 13

Settling in Vancouver
1964 onwards

With Jeremy now three, we flew in a Constellation to Montreal in September 1964, where we were met by and stayed with Joe and Margaret for a few days while I bought a 1960 Meteor, a big underpowered station wagon to drive across Canada to Vancouver. It was good to catch up with these friends again, and we were sure that one day they would get out to Vancouver.

The drive was a five-day slog, four times the length of England, as we passed through Ottawa, Algonquin Park and Sudbury to Sault Ste. Marie. Up to Soo, we had cruised through vast areas of tall trees on both sides of the road, and these cut out any long views. In the town, we had a look at the Soo locks, and a quick look at the town, especially the Windsor Hotel where I had stayed. Then it was on to Thunder Bay, Winnipeg, Regina and Calgary, finally arriving in Vancouver. Whenever the weather was clear and we found a nice camp site, we three slept out in our Meteor Monster, one of the advantages of a large station wagon. The vast immensity of the country — as daily we were looking at a straight road in front of us disappearing over the far horizon — often caused me about mid-morning to consider, as usual, a short kip.

Having been in contact with WEL, I found they were ready to accept me back into the company. It was good to know I had a job available, having been laid off in the past when the market slowed down.

I had been investing in various mines while away, and we were fortunate enough to have built a fund to buy a house. While we rented an apartment, we searched for a house with various agents showing us houses for sale. We eventually found one in a cul-de-sac near Edgemont Village on the North Shore close to shops and a school for Jeremy. It had a basement, three bedrooms, kitchen, and a bathroom. Importantly, the back garden faced south and had a bit of a view of Lions Gate Bridge. We obtained a 5% $8,000 mortgage on the $14,000 for the 900 sq. ft. house. We had it for 20 years.

After we lived there a while, I realized we had no direct link to the garden except through the side, front and back doors. I realized I needed doors directly into the garden through a balcony from the south-facing living room. I discussed the problem with Heather. Then, one Saturday morning at 5 a.m. I took the windows out and cut part of the wall out, and now had a complete opening to the garden, a wonderful feeling. By Sunday evening I had side windows back in, along with two swing doors, which would open outwards over the balcony — the next job, for an even better feeling. I went back to the office on Monday for a physical rest. Later, with the balcony and the steps down into the garden, it was delightful to sit outside and enjoy the sun. Anni, who worked for me as a drafting technician when I was on the Port Moody project, and her engineering husband Jens, came and helped build the balcony.

With a solid job and a comfortable house, we felt it was time for Jeremy to have some company and by 21 March 1965, Heather had delivered our beautiful Erica at the same Grace Hospital and by the same doctor. It was lucky that we took a trial run a few days earlier to know the way there because I had forgotten it. We loved our new addition and how she and Jeremy reacted together. The same pram and box arrangement now worked for Erica. At that time Heather did not need to work, and it was a period of halcyon days, days with no rush to get anything done but days when living was just calm and relaxed, enjoying our new house and our children. Wonderful.

As the days passed, we started thinking about getting a sailboat again and eventually bought, along with the Blankensteins who had returned from Australia, a popular and locally designed 26-foot plywood Thunderbird sailboat called

Kolus. On many Friday evenings, Heather would meet me at work with food for the weekend and she would drive the family to the boat at Thunderbird Marina while I changed into boat gear. Before the evening was out, we would be up the coast and into some quiet bay absorbing life on the sea until Sunday night. We have such a marvellous marine environment with many islands where we can sample nature, beaches and water all day long, maybe running along a beach in the evening and leaving phosphorescent footsteps in the sand. We might even watch young Jeremy peeing into the sea at night, making phosphorescent lines.

At home, it was wonderful to watch our children growing up. Now we had Erica pushing her trolley from one end of the living room to the other while we encouraged her. Anything sensitive or breakable had already been lifted to a safer height, first for Jeremy and now for her. She was and still is a determined girl. When I had taken time off later to enter the real estate business while Heather was working, I often took her to Joyce Reindeer's, our friend down the street, for babysitting. Having just dressed Erica, I might go to the bathroom and when I returned, she would be standing there naked saying, "I'm not going." With my schedule about to be shot, I'd pick her up "as is" with her clothes and thrust them into Joyce's hands saying, "Sorry about this but I have an appointment." Joyce always had a great sense of humour and would just laugh. Once when our two families and children were together having lunch in Sewell's at Horseshoe Bay, Jeremy, shaking the ketchup bottle, did not realize the lid was off and the red sauce went flying all over us and other people. Suddenly there was an embarrassing silence for a moment, and then Joyce roared out laughing. Then everyone laughed while the owner hurried over with a cloth and started wiping the mess off people. We had met Joyce and her husband Lewis at the local childcare centre and had enjoyable skiing outings and times with them.

My mum came again in 1966 for two months and this time friends Charlie and Sue Hills kindly lent us their VW camper. We drove up to Prince Rupert and came back by ferry and down Vancouver Island. On the way, we stopped to see the famous

Williams Lake Stampede. She could not believe we were stamped on the back of our hand when we paid the entrance fee or having to step over a drunk lying in the entranceway. Neither on the following morning, could she believe seeing the number of bodies lying around the site, most probably with hangovers. We enjoyed all the rodeo, cowgirl, bull and wagon race events, a real Canadian scene.

Further north we stayed at a campsite on Francois Lake in a primitive log cabin — primitive because it only had cold water with a log fire for cooking. Mum definitely thought it was the backwoods. We took her out on a small power boat to look at places around the lake, but we all started laughing so much when trying to get her off, that Heather and I actually rolled her onto the dock. Lucky she still had long trousers!

When I took the boat keys back to the owner, I saw a man looking down at a large animal skull. I said, "That looks interesting."

He asked, "Do you know what it is?"

"Yes, it is an herbivorous animal because you can see all the back teeth are ground flat by what it eats."

"So, if you know these things, can you tell me what animals these come from?" and with that he pulled out from his pocket, to my utter amazement, a number of different round turds, one of which was a dark colour. I studied them for a moment and in a serious voice said, "Well, there is no doubt they all come from the same animals, elk, but I suspect one has been taking All Bran."

There was a moment's silence as he absorbed this, and then he looked up and saw my big grin. "I must tell my wife this," he said, laughing, and rushed off. When I told my mum this story, she could not stop laughing.

We were so pleased that my mum had been able to get a couple of trips out to see us, Jeremy and our newly born Erica, because it was only six months later, we were saddened to hear from my brothers that she had suddenly been taken ill with cancer. After a short stay in hospital, she passed away in January 1967. Heather and I were much set back at her loss, while I was thinking there was just me and my three brothers left in the family, but slowly this feeling eased as we kept referring to her past trips and the fun we had with her. She had been a wonderful, loving person and mum. Her gravestone lies in the churchyard at the west end of Banstead Village.

As Jeremy and Erica moved out of kindergarten and into school, they started developing friendships. Erica became almost inseparable from Karen Jacobson who lived down the road below us and then one day the friendship ended; we never knew why but even some adults are like that. The two girls were really horse-mad and preferred model horses to Barbie dolls. Erica went to horse ranches where she looked after the horses and took guests riding.

Jeremy used to be on the school basketball and volleyball teams and was pretty athletic. He was impressive in the high jump, and I was surprised one day to see he had changed from his normal style to the Fosbury Flop. When jumping, especially at the Empire Stadium, he seemed to wait for the crowd to quieten. I always wondered if this helped put pressure on him to jump higher. His closest friend and teammate, was Dennis Lefeaux. When they were older, we were impressed when they started leaving early for school to study (so they said). We learned a long time later from a girl that they came early to watch the cheerleaders practicing in the gym — and we thought they were so keen on doing well.

Naturally, we always attended the teacher's report meetings and tried to support any weak subject with discussions over dinner. I am sure they both did better than I did at school.

At work there was no rest as I was immediately put in charge of starting and running an estimating department for costing works required for mines. There was always pressure to get results needed for feasibility studies so an owner could decide whether he or his company wished to go ahead with a project. If he did, there would be more work, and I might be handling one or even three different mines at a time.

My first job overseas (1967) occurred when the company was

asked to make a study for four ports (Iquitos, Puerto Maldonado, Pucallpa and Ucayali) on the Amazon River and its tributaries. It was for the Department of Marine Transportation, Peru. I was elected to manage the study and, although I knew a bit of Spanish, I was provided with a Spanish mining technician to help out. On our overnight flight to Lima, Peru, I had a bit of a shock when coming back from the forward toilet because, seeing so many passengers wearing black eye shields so that they could sleep, the cabin looked like a pirate's den.

We visited the client's huge office and were introduced to his deputy who would travel with us. The next day we were gaining height in an old Dakota to cross the pass in the Andes Mountains to Pucallpa in the jungle, known as the Oriente. We were sitting in two single lines with our backs to the outside with freight tied down in the centre aisle. When the steward came through with a number of tubes over his arm, I wondered what they were for until I saw him putting these "hookah" tubes into slots near us, so we could hold the tube under our noses to breathe oxygen. It was crude but effective; smoking was not advised. The mountains loomed over us and seemed too close as we just cleared the pass.

Flying down over the jungle, I was impressed by the number of river bends, bow lakes and parts of old rivers that inundated the surface along with bends that were just about to meet each other and form another bow lake. Apart from where the river was actually flowing, there were other signs that this had happened many times in the past. It was as if the fingers of a giant hand had scraped across the land surface in different directions, showing where the river had been thousands of years ago. In Pucallpa, the river elevation is around 500 feet, and the river mouth is some 4,000 miles away. Therefore, the average slope is approximately 1 in 40,000. It is a wonder it flows at all when we use slopes of 1 in 100 to drain our balconies or flat areas that often seem too flat for drainage.

I examined the four sites and selected a port site at Pucallpa. When I came back with my boss six months later after the high-water season, we found nearly 300 feet of the site had disappeared. We could not figure out why and needed an immediate aerial survey to find out what the river was doing. A military survey would take at least several months to obtain, so we hired the local missionary's four-seater plane. We removed a door so I could be strapped in on the floor and have my head and camera outside the plane to take a series of pictures. So, at 4,000 feet, I moved into position with the wind whistling past my head and started taking pictures of the river. It was pretty scary, but it got the job done.

The new pictures indicated the natural movement of the river, which normally cuts through softer ground, was being restricted by some harder soil. It had caused an increase in the current, which had removed a large chunk of the bank. Calculations showed that once the bend moved past this hard point it would continue moving, and in an estimated five years, it was unlikely the river would be near the town. This is indeed what happened after 10 years. Iquitos was a developed port where we recommended modernization. Here 2,000-tonne ships from the English Booth Line came all the way up the river, probably around 2,000 miles. The other two ports required minimal installations to handle the local river craft.

When I had completed the site work, my client insisted I could not leave Peru until I had seen Machu Picchu. "I will take you there this weekend," he said. I was absolutely staggered by this kind offer, especially since I liked the client. From Cusco (11,000 ft) we took a train to the site station, Aguas Calientes, climbed into an old truck, and while standing up holding onto a crossbar, were taken up the hill on a steep, multi-zigzag gravel road to the hotel.

There were fewer than fifty visitors at the site, and the view across the many old stone buildings at 8,000 ft was breathtaking. It was the Lost City of the Incas built in the 15th century. Some of the buildings had vertical trapezoidal slots for viewpoints, below which the land was terraced down steep slopes. No roofs were left. The many, even large, stones had no mortar between the absolutely smooth joints, an outstanding feature. As we roamed around, I had to wonder how all this had been planned and built, let alone why. After looking at the ruins, I said to my client, "I am going see if I can climb up that peak," Huayna Picchu, which is 950 ft higher, and he replied, "I'll be down at the Temple of Virgins," and we laughed when I said, "Watch out."

There were no charges or warnings at what seemed to be a path. Not knowing it is often called the "Death Hike" or "Stairs of Death" I struggled up narrow, irregular, stepped paths, often quite steep, sometimes with a fearful drop on one side, to finally ease my way under a large rock and onto the summit. Some of the drop-offs at the side of the pathways were pretty scary. I was alone on the top. It was a moment of pure isolation and silence which I enjoyed. The 360-degree view across the surrounding mountains made me wonder if other unique sites like this existed. Down below, I could hardly see anyone in the buildings or on the steep terraced slopes. Way down in the valley, the brown Urubamba River flowed on its way to join the Amazon. I would have loved to stay longer looking at the mountains around me but went down and found my client.

As we motored down the zigzag road with local kids running down the fall-line with their hands out for coins, I thanked my client profusely for his kindness in showing me the site. It is now a World Heritage site, and in 2013, 1.2 million visitors passed through turnstile gates. There is concern about site deterioration due to the number of visitors. I was lucky to be there before it became such a popular place. My CEO received a thank-you letter "for the magnificent presentation of the report."

I was so influenced by the use of arches everywhere in Peru that when I returned home, I changed rectangular door openings into arches, which we loved, in our main hallway; it certainly improved the look of the place, and our friends and neighbours were impressed by the change.

Another job soon followed in South America, this time in Bolivia. In 1968 WEL was building a lead-zinc mine there for a major US steel company. Some problems were developing and I was asked to go and sort them out. It was a rushed task, and I went with a senior partner flying to Miami and then straight onto

La Paz at over 11,000 ft where we arrived late in the day. At 5 a.m. the next morning, a jeep took us up to the mine at over 12,000 ft. On the way, I told my VP that statistically, one of us was going to have a problem with altitude sickness, because we were not acclimatizing properly. This did not worry him as he was only staying a day.

After spending the day inspecting progress at the mine at even higher altitudes, I started my evening dinner, only to find I had a distinct lack of interest in eating. Soon, I was outside throwing up. All through the long night, I found myself sitting up, rocking on my bed, holding onto my head, wondering if the splitting, hammering pain would ever go away. In the morning, I was taken back down to La Paz, where I reclined in my hotel bed for the next few days just eating a bun a day while the VP returned to Vancouver. I'm sure some friends think I have not yet recovered.

When I returned to work on the site, I had to deal with the US company representative for whom nothing was right, and who wanted to close the job down. I managed to stop that and sort out the other problems. He was an unpleasant person who, the moment I arrived for breakfast, always challenged me about what was being done or not done. Finally, I told him I preferred to have my meal first and then I would be ready for his questions.

One evening at dinner, a couple arrived and soon waiters were serving them, and flames from dishes they had ordered could be seen. He asked, "Isn't that the couple from your office?" and when I affirmed this, he replied, "Do you realize that's my money going up in flames?" There was no humour in this question as he was not a charming type. I later heard that he died falling down a lift shaft in Rio de Janeiro when a back panel failed. He was the type of person who could undermine your confidence, but not mine, just by his aggressiveness.

While I enjoyed all the colourful sights and ways of Bolivia, it was nice to be home again and out on our boat where peace reigned, well, at least most of the time. *Kolus* provided us with four years of happy summer sailing. After two years, we bought out our partner and arranged the layout as we wished. We loved exploring all the bays, islands and marinas on our friendly west coast. Sometimes, I would be up and motoring or sailing *Kolus* in the early morning while Heather and the kids were still asleep. In this way, we avoided the time spent getting somewhere and were always close to a beach when they woke up. They could take the dinghy and have fun learning to row it, while I had a line to it, in case they had a problem. Often when it rained, there might be a leak with water dripping down on where they slept. Our quick fix was to take a plywood panel from some other part of the boat and lay it over them, so the water was directed to the side of the hull and they kept dry — primitive but effective.

When not sailing, we would be hiking on the local mountains with Erica in my rucksack, and when they were both older, urging them along the trail with encouraging remarks like, "We'll be there over the next rise and the view is superb." This did not always stop the groans as we plodded upwards. Now Jeremy at 56 runs daily in the mountains with his new partner Jenni, and Erica, living in England with her family, runs and boxes regularly.

We used to hike a lot with our children but I would often hike alone. If the weather looked good for the next day, I would make my sandwiches the night before. Up at 5 a.m., and if the weather was good, I would be gone, hiking up the local 5,000–6000 ft mountains Harvey, Brunswick, Grouse, or even the Lions. There would be a quiet, satisfying remoteness at the top and fun when striding down, telling hikers coming up in the heat of the day how far it was to the top. One time on the top when having a kip, I was woken by hail falling on my face. I only went to the top of the Lions once when going with Swiss friends who used a rope to help me over the last bit, as it was too scary for me. In later years there seemed to be more bears, even cougars, and I was not so happy hiking alone. The safe rule is always to hike with someone who cannot run as fast as you!

Once with Pierre Bourquin, Ken Farquharson, Herbert Eigermann and two others, we hiked up Mount Baker, 10,750 ft. We camped out at the Kulshan Cabin at 5,000 ft. At 4:30 a.m. we started out and saw high on the mountain what looked like glow-worms but they were groups already on the move with their headlights on. Six hours later, having cramponed our way up with an increasing number of stops and a growing headache, we collapsed on the top and noticed a slight drift of smoke coming from one end of the peak, perhaps a minor fumarole.

On the way down, we came to a crevasse where a skier had not stopped in time and had fallen in. Since we were the only group with ropes, one person volunteered to be lowered down to help her. Ken and I decided to run down, report the problem, pick up the stretcher from the Kulshan Cabin, and bring it back up. On the way back up and pretty exhausted by now, I was happy as a guy coming down took it from us, hoisted it over his head and started trotting back up the mountain. Now how did he have the energy to do this? It was apparently needed as I heard she was brought down on the stretcher.

In the following week, Herbert, a Swiss engineer who worked for me, went back to the crevasse because although they had pulled the skier out, the skis had been left behind. I did not think it worth going all the way back and into a crevasse for somebody else's skis. I heard the following story: his two friends lowered Herbert down, but he could not see any skis and told them to pull him up. He was standing on a 4 x 6 ft ice shelf in the vertical face of the crevasse wall. His two friends found they did not have enough strength to pull him up, possibly because of the friction of the rope on the snow at the top of the crevasse. They lowered their jackets and food down and said they were going for extra help. Ten hours later, they returned with help and pulled him out. In that time, Herbert said he had been doing knee bends to try and keep warm, had watched the moon pass overhead, and was hoping that the continuous vibrations and thundering noises would not cause the crevasse to close up. He had a weak heart.

On another occasion, Herbert, George Forrestal, and four others and I were on an overnight ski traverse from the Diamond Head cabin to Garibaldi Rail Station. We were going to cross the side of Garibaldi Mountain, down the Warren Glacier at Table

Mountain, cross the Garibaldi Lake and hike down to the rail station. After hiking into Diamond Head Lodge, we stayed the night and left early after breakfast. Six hours later, we were still hiking up but when mist and clouds closed in, I said to Herbert, "Do you know where we are?" to which he replied, "I know exactly... uh-oh, there is a crevasse just ahead." Why do I put my faith in the Swiss?

We agreed to stop and put our tents up for the night or until the weather cleared. Next morning it was clear, so we roped up again and skied on. George, who'd had a cold night, did not wish to go further and decided to ski back. We thought he would be okay and let him go on his own — not a good policy. He was okay, but we heard that when the Diamond Head people saw him coming down on his own, they thought there had been an accident. Finally, we got going down past Table Mountain and onto the lake. It was a long four-mile hike across the lake, with me hoping not to hear any cracking ice sounds as I think we were probably the last people to cross the lake that spring before the ice melted. We finally reached the end of the lake, hiked down the Barrier where the occasional lava rock could be seen falling on the cliff face, and hiked the three hours out to the train station. It took me a week to recover.

In 1969, I was scheduled to look into two possible jobs in India and Cairo. Since I would be travelling via London, I decided Heather should come and we would see our family and also our friends Norman and Gloria Elliott, who were still living in the UK. While there, I learned the Cairo prospect had been postponed and that Norman and Gloria were driving to Venice to meet up with Jamie Davidson whom we knew was on a year's sabbatical with his wife, Patsy. Knowing I now had a week spare before heading to India, we asked if we could join them on their drive to Venice. They thought it a good idea, and a couple of days later Heather and I booked into the hotel where the others were staying on a package deal.

With a bit of fun in mind, we planned that when Jamie and Patsy arrived, Norman would invite them into their room and order champagne. I would bring it up, dressed in a waiter's borrowed coat wearing a cap, with a fag hanging out of my mouth. The hotel staff thought this quite funny. Armed with a tray of glasses and bottle, with a hotel napkin over my arm, I knocked at the door, found it to be the wrong one and made my excuses. I wondered what they thought. At the right door, I knocked again and Norman opened it, and I walked in with my head down. My plan if not recognized was to give Patsy a pat on her behind, but Jamie suddenly yelled out, "Christ, it's Patrick."

We had a splendid two days there with them and then Heather and I moved on to Rome where she took a plane back to Germany to see Roger in the army, and I flew to India. While in Venice, Heather and I often wondered why we seemed to have the better room of the three with a nice balcony overlooking a canal. When I got the bill we knew why, because we were not on their package and had a deluxe room. I realized I would be eating sandwiches for the next few months.

Later we had a "return match" in Vancouver when the Davidsons invited us to dinner at a hotel downtown. When we arrived, Jamie insisted we put our coats in the cloakroom, and as I was wondering why he was so insistent, Norman, with a big grin, popped out to take them. He had just flown over from England for business. Surprise, surprise.

Although I enjoyed working in the mining business, I decided I wanted a more civil engineering orientated company. In 1969, I joined up with a local company, Swan Wooster Engineering (SWE), after a lunch meeting at the Royal Vancouver Yacht Club with two of their managers. My first task was working as the project engineer on the Stage 1 development of the Westshore Bulk Coal Terminal south of Vancouver, and in its later Stage 2, as the project manager working with a major engineering company in San Mateo. It was an interesting design-build project dealing with and learning all about new equipment to unload and ship out 20 million tons of coal a year. In between other projects and feasibility studies over the next years, I managed to get unpaid time off, allowing me to work on building my sailboat.

CHAPTER 14

Building our Dream Boat
1970–76

We were enjoying our sailing so much that Heather and I started thinking about sailing offshore. We had heard and read so much about this kind of trip that we thought we should undertake one. Our 26 ft Thunderbird boat was not big enough, as we reckoned we would need a forty-footer, but we did not have the money for a new one or even a used one. Designers did not help as their plans alone were far too expensive. Our enquiries in 1970 led us to meeting up with Charlie Kennedy, a South African who was building his broad-beam 45 ft boat in his garden to his own design, and we liked it. He and his wife, Liv, became long-term friends. We had met them at Paul and Doreen's new house when the Kennedys had just returned from a world sailing trip in his self-built 37 ft boat. We met Paul and Doreen at the Capilano Tennis Club. They were also building a Thunderbird boat.

A month later, Charlie called us saying the jigs for a 42 ft boat were for sale and thought this size would be good for us. Six airline pilots had designed this 42 ft x 12 ft beam boat. One, Jim Innes, who created the Victoria to Maui race, wanted his boat early and had built his own boat by a one-off method, while the others built theirs through use of moulds for the hull and deck built by the DeKleer Brothers, boat builders.

The jigs were ten wooden frames that provided the shape of the hull every 4 ft. We immediately bought them from Jim, such an active guy, and within a month had the full size of the boat-shape laid out upside-down in our small back garden. It looked immense, and I wondered if I could finish it without blowing my budget to pieces. After first getting my local neighbours signed up for two years to allow me to build, I finished it in the remarkably short time of three years. I had made a fiberglass airex-cored hull and balsa-cored deck, finished the carpentry inside, and installed the engine, lights and all fittings. All this was done with Heather's help when we sometimes glassed the hull before I went to work at 7 a.m. — definitely a "do it now" project.

In the early stages of building, I changed the design, although I was not a boat designer. I worked at this in the evenings, after I had stopped any physical work and the children had gone to bed. I added another 6 ft on the mast height, another 1,000 lb of lead in the keel, shortened the keel length and modernized its shape, modified the spade rudder to include a skeg for better steering control, modernized the conventional stern to a reverse stern (this gave me an extra foot of space in the boat) and many other minor changes. I bought much of the expensive equipment such as mast, engine, winches and cables with other boat builders so we could get discounts. Sounds simple? But don't try it unless you're motivated and have a very positive partner like Heather.

I always worked whenever I could, and any work Heather did during the day was a tremendous lift of spirit for me. For instance, I might tack into place a bulkhead with advice to Heather on how to fully fiberglass it into place, and it might be done when I returned home. Or she would just clear up the mess I left. One night, I went to bed happy that I had successfully pop-rivetted the sail track onto the aluminum mast that evening. When my eyes opened in the morning, the ghastly realization came that I had not installed the electrical cable for the upper anchor light under the track. Shoot! That night I had to drill out all the pop rivets and start over. The mistake made me realize I must be more careful and not, for instance, cut expensive teak late at night, when tired, in case I made a mismeasurement.

There were two key emotional moments during building. First, as my selected crane operator lifted the hull up and carefully rolled it over upright in the slings, there she was looking very sleek with me probably looking smug. Seeing this huge hull hanging above me, I wondered how I had done this. The emotion increased as it was lifted over the house and lowered onto the prepared chocks in the driveway. That night we had the first of many parties celebrating the various stages of building. The next day was one of rest and recovery. We had been going five months.

Second was the melting and pouring of the lead keel. At first light, on the morning of the 8,000 lb lead pour, I got the 200 lb of coke lit. Its heat was increased by blowing a good blast of oxygen from our vacuum cleaner through a steel tube into the coke lying between metal drums holding the lead. I also had six large gas torches heating the sides of the drums. Our insurance company had not been advised of this activity. Experience from others had indicated in about four hours the lead would be molten and ready to pour.

An hour later, my elderly neighbour, balancing on his walking stick, leaned over the fence and in a querulous voice, asked with good humour, "Er, er, Mr. Hill, how have you managed to get an industrial zoning for your property?"

After a further two hours, willing friends (carefully selected, mind you) had arrived to help. A fireman and a sailor (Bob Lefeaux, father of Dennis, Jeremy's friend), a doctor and a sailor (Paul Watson), an engineer and my work colleague (Bill McLachlan), a labour negotiator, and a wannabe sailor-carpenter friend, Paul Jakobsen (father of Erica's friend, Karen). When I took Paul Jakobsen out on an overnight race, he was so sick that his wife thanked me afterwards because his sailing desire had evaporated, and he no longer wanted to buy a sailboat.

Now the lead looked molten and another moment of truth had arrived, while I sweated and wondered if the whole process would work. I broke the seal on a pipe leading from the drums into the concrete mould I had made and out poured red hot lead. What a relief! I felt like a medieval alchemist.

We called the boat *Sky One Hundred* because Erica, when wanting to say something big, might say, "I love you, Mummy, one hundred and the sky." The use of the number one hundred is maybe why she has her own business as an accountant now. A year later with the painting done, engine, cables, steering and innards installed, a truck arrived, slid its trailer carefully under the boat and towed it out into the street while neighbours stood around watching. Some clapped, probably realizing that peace and quietness would now return. It was towed to Mosquito Creek for its launch, while Sam and Jill, our marine friends, took movie shots of the trip. After a dose of champagne, it slid into the sea while being photographed by the *North Shore Shopper* (now the *North Shore News*). There was a big celebration with many friends. We enjoyed the boat for the next 22 years.

It was also a very uplifting moment for Heather and myself after 6,000 hours of work while I was working as an engineer over the three years. The 2,000 hours a year is the equivalent of another full-time job, so I am so fortunate to have such a willing and keen partner providing solid support. During building, we continued to have parties with other boat builders at every key construction event. At the last party, I gave presents to our long-suffering neighbours — their wrapped tools they had lent me from time to time. It was well worth all the toil of building it, and I still wonder where all the motivation and energy came from. While building, visitors who were positive were welcome but others were eased away. I did not want to be told how much work was needed or that sailing offshore could be dangerous.

In 1972 during the building, Helen and Chris, Heather's parents, came for a visit to see us and the kids. In their four-week stay, we think they fell in love with Vancouver and being in a new environment. Perhaps they were like Heather and me in our early days, looking for a new adventure. We were living in our *Brantwood* home, which was not big but the balcony faced south and we were close to Edgemont Village. We actually got Chris on my skis once down at Mount Baker.

I believe during and after this trip, they started thinking about emigrating here. This was probably because Roger, their son, an officer in the paratroopers, spent much of his time overseas in strategic locations and was not conveniently located in the UK. After they were back in England, we heard they were applying to immigrate, had been accepted, were selling their house and were coming by ship through the Panama. It was all exciting news, especially for Jeremy and Erica who would have grandparents living close by. After their arrival, they stayed with us while they searched for a place to live and for jobs. Helen found a job with the *North Shore Shopper* in the advertising department and started to get to know many people. Chris found a job with a bank delivering documents around town, a nice physical job instead of his previous desk job. Chris also helped in the building of *Sky One Hundred*, and they were able to join us on many sailing trips, which the kids loved.

Helen and Chris were such an active couple that they were like our friends and fended for themselves at all times, making their own friends, and finding their own place to live. They both played bowls, took up golf and came hiking with us at any time. Chris even played snooker with the mayor. Helen took up the analysis of handwriting. She was so good at this that I used to bring home written notes from people in my office, and in ten minutes she was telling me their basic characteristics. It was so revealing it was scary. She told us that sometimes, at lawyer conventions, they would line up to hear her views on their writing. However, I never let her see my writing. She also took up cross-country skiing and painting. It was so sad to see this energetic couple slowing down as they entered their latter days. Towards the end, they went into homes to be fully looked after and finally they passed away, Helen in 1995 and Chris in 2003, after many happy years with us in Canada. I could not believe that while writing obituaries for this wonderful couple, I needed a private place at my office to handle such an emotional wrench.

CHAPTER 15

Sailing to the South Seas
and Alaska
1977–78

After the 1974 launch of *Sky One Hundred*, we had many local trips across Georgia Strait and up the coast. This was the biggest boat I had sailed, and I just loved its power easing through the waves. Cruising into different bays we had not seen before was always exciting, along with appreciative comments from strangers on the finished look of our boat. Particularly when sailing, I liked shaving in the morning looking through the head window at the passing mountains and coast views while Heather and the kids kept her going. It was such a feeling of freedom.

After a sailing season, we all decided to sail *Sky One Hundred* around Vancouver Island to practice offshore sailing. This did not happen because on the way when we docked at Squirrel Cove, Lasqueti Island there was an accident. Jeremy and Erica had dinghied across to a small island to play, and we suddenly heard a scream and crying. Jeremy called out that a log had rolled on her foot and there was a lot of blood. With Erica still screaming, I immediately told him to put her in the dinghy and bring her back. It was bad. The front pad of her foot was hanging down, partially sheared off. While Heather held her, I bound her damaged foot for protection and to minimise the blood flow. I then ran to find a local with a car. I was fortunate, and he took us all up to False Bay. Here a waiting rescue boat took Heather with Erica across to Nanaimo to be met by an ambulance and rushed to the hospital. I sighed with relief that this happened so quickly. The local who drove his car got in such a panic driving (perhaps seeing the blood) I had to tell him to calm down before he rolled his car. Jeremy and I went back with him for our boat and took it to

Nanaimo. Erica was in the hospital for four weeks, while we were allowed to stay at Nanaimo YC for free, visiting her every day. The doctor did a very good job on her seriously damaged foot, putting it pretty well right again.

After racing *Sky One Hundred*, winning some races, including the annual Straits race, and exploring the west coast islands for three years, we were happy the way our boat functioned and decided to take an offshore trip. In 1977, Heather and I asked the heads of Jeremy and Erica's schools if we could take them out of school for a year while we went sailing to the South Seas. They expressed enthusiasm for this idea especially when we said we wanted correspondence courses for them so they would not fall behind.

I asked for a year's leave of absence from my boss at SWE but had to drop my key project manager job of the main expansion at the Westshore Coal Terminal project where construction was just about to start. Even our American client could live with this dream, giving me a farewell lunch when I left, and I don't think he was a sailor. I was sorry to leave the job but I had been anticipating the trip ever since we built *Sky One Hundred.* I also felt there was always work available.

Our trip involved cruising down the Oregon Coast to San Francisco, Mexico, three weeks' sail to the Marquesas Islands, and then on to the Tuamotus, Tahiti, Huahine, Raiatea and Tahaa, and the mystical Bora Bora. We would return via the Hawaiian Islands, across the north Pacific to Glacier Bay and back to Vancouver down the Inside Passage within a year. Jeremy was 16 and Erica 12. It turned out to be an exciting, enlightening and highly enjoyable 15,000 mile, 14-month adventure with our family. It is described in my book titled, *So Where Do You Go at Night?* since many people do not know what an ocean is like and often asked these questions. Did we drop anchor at night? Did we stop at a marina? No, we just kept going.

On the trip, we experienced moments of extreme excitement, concern and pleasure while meeting islanders and other yachties, interwoven with crossing oceans and living at close quarters. One worry was looking up at the big following waves on the Oregon coast much bigger than anything we had ever sailed in. We often wondered if the next one would drop into the cockpit. Surfing down these waves became exciting and soon had Heather, Jeremy and I fighting to take the wheel to see who could get the fastest surfing speed out of the boat, just touching 15 knots.

Closing in on the first island in the Marquesas after twenty days sailing from Manzanillo, Mexico, seeing nothing but sea, while plotting our course by sextant — GPS was not available yet — I was beginning to worry that if we did not see an island, where the heck would we go? It's a lonely place out there. One boat did radio us, asking us to work out their position if they gave us their data, as they were lost. Finally, we saw a cloud that did not move. It was over our target island.

We enjoyed the wonderful warmth and friendliness of the Tahitians, learning to dance Tahitian style, salivating over their poisson cru dish, the colourful fish, the wonderful clarity of the blue-green waters inside the reefs and were sad when we left Bora Bora. In Uturoa, we really appreciated being welcomed to Jean Yves' house, meeting his family and visiting his plantation. These are things we will never forget.

Our 18-day voyage up to Hilo on the Big Island seemed to be a beat the whole way and was an uncomfortable trip. Three days out of Hilo, we could not see the island or its highest peak, Mauna Loa, at 14,000 ft because of a dense sea mist. We could not see the horizon or the sun so could not do any celestial navigation. We could hear the Hilo radio broadcast and headed west in what we thought was the right direction. Surprisingly, we suddenly saw houses high up in the mist on the mountainside and voila the Hilo harbour entrance was in front of us. What a relief!

After two days, we pushed on to the friendly Ali Wai Yacht Club, Oahu, and were thrilled to meet up with Colin Hempsall, a fellow West Vancouver Yacht Club member who had just sailed in single-handedly from Samoa. We had last seen his boat disappearing over the horizon westwards when we started sailing south for Mexico.

On a night sail from Oahu to Kauai, we were a bit worried about the strength of the northeast trade winds as we left the shelter of Oahu. An hour later we had a mighty crash, and *Sky One Hundred* was thrown on her side by a big wave. Heather was jetted out of her bunk onto me, sleeping on the floor, while Jeremy, on watch, ended up on the back of the cockpit seats. This meant our boat was thrown on its side with the mast after lying on the sea, slowly coming vertical with the weight of the keel. This was the worst experience we had at sea. I grabbed my lifejacket and rushed onto the deck, disconnected our self-steering gear and carefully steered by hand, watching the moonlight glimmer on the top of the big waves coming up behind and lifting us up, until we got into calmer waters and into Hanalei Bay. Here, many boats were finishing their cruise and heading back to Seattle or Vancouver.

Halfway up to Glacier Bay, we met up with the Canadian weather ship in the middle of the north Pacific. The captain told us we were the first sailboat they had seen up there in five years. He also told us there was someone on their ship that knew us from our tennis club. That small world again. I might also confirm that six months before writing this, a man taking our lines as we were docking up the coast said, "Hello, Patrick." I replied in a surprised voice, "How do you know me?" He said, "I met you when you came into Glacier Bay in 1978 in your nice boat, *Sky One Hundred*." "Holy Smoke!" I said, "That was 39 years ago."

Recently at my eye specialist, a lady said, "Hello, Patrick." I replied, "How do you know me?" She said, "I've read two of your books." Well, that was a thrill.

We had asked Helen and Chris if they would like to join us in Glacier Bay, so there was tremendous excitement as we approached the official dock and could see them waving to us. At about the same time, I had just been in ham radio contact with our South Seas buddy boat, *Restless Wind*, heading back to Seattle. When we said goodbye to them in Hanalei Bay, Kauai, after sailing together for a year, they kindly rowed over and presented us with a bottle of champagne. What a swell gesture!

We were awed by the raw glacial ice scenes in Glacier Bay, some we could not get within two miles of because of the brash ice covering the sea. It encouraged us to organize a "do it soon" plan to sail along the Alaskan coast five years later.

The building of the boat and our delightful trip was only possible through the super positive help and encouragement from Heather at all times. I am fortunate to have such a lovable partner.

On our return in August 1978, Jeremy and Erica rejoined their friends at school in the same classes, their target while away, but with a whole new perspective on life and increased maturity. For Heather and me, being in such close association with them both 24/7 on our trip had been a magical time.

Jeremy had one year of school left. At his graduation, we were surprised when he told the audience he was going to be an accountant. He started work after school at Kitsilano Marine store in June 1979. In the same year, with his off-shore experience, he was invited to join a 34 ft boat with five other crew members to be navigator on the 16-day Victoria-Maui boat race, and sail the boat back for the owner, a long-time friend of ours, Darryl Delmotte. It was a rough sail back with one person being briefly swept overboard by a wave and quickly rescued.

By the fall of 1981, he had enlisted in UBC Sciences to train as an engineer. He became so fed up with the number of Chinese students there, speaking their own language all the time, that by spring 1982 he quit. He then did a two-year accounting finance program at Capilano University. He worked for a while in a bar in North Vancouver to help pay for school. Heather and I were very pleased that he later joined up with a work acquaintance, Aussie Murray Ashworth, and they started their own business. They formed a recreational boat repair shop on Granville Island in 1984 for two years. But with the introduction of too many restrictions, they moved on, taking their skills to open a boat repair shop at Thunderbird Marina, which they ran successfully for five years until Jeremy sold his share in 1991. When Jeremy first brought Murray up to our house, he looked at a picture of our boat and immediately said, "I painted your boat," which he had done two years after we had returned from the South Seas. At the time I had silently cursed him, as he would not touch it unless I gave it another sanding with finer sandpaper. He was that kind of perfectionist.

On 28 May 1992, Jeremy and Ramy were married at our Overstone house in West Vancouver in a simple ceremony. Dennis, one of the three best men, provided a huge sail that we could use to cover the guests between the house and the trees on the other side of the lawn in case it rained. Michael, my eldest nephew, came over from Regina, helped to put lights up and serve the drinks. I had a shock when Jeremy's friend in charge of drinks told me about 15 minutes after the ceremony was over that the first barrel of beer was finished. Ramy's family came, along with Jeremy's friends and our friends, Jamie and Patsy and Norman and Gloria and many others. It did not rain and everything went off well with good speeches and much amusement.

Later in January 1994, Jeremy was asked to go to Tangu, China just outside Tianjin on the coast, and work for an old customer in supervising the construction of his 33 m steel schooner in a state-run shipyard with over 6,000 employees building freighters. This lasted only three months as the workers and management of the shipyard were, in Jeremy's words "unscrupulous at best," and the project ground to a halt. He said it was the filthiest environment he had ever experienced and looking at his pictures, I agreed with him. In fact, when he showed their Chinese translator where the boat was going in the South Seas with blue skies and seas, she promptly said, "That propaganda — all sky grey."

In the fall of 1994, Jeremy's wife, Ramy, was offered a national sales manager position based in Toronto. As they were still young and childless, they went for it. They joined us in Buffalo for a weekend when we sailed down to the Bahamas. On returning from this trip, Riley, their daughter, was born on 22 February 1998. We encouraged them later to return to Vancouver, which they happily did. They thought Toronto was a nice place, but they didn't want to live there permanently. In the spring of 1999, they bought a house in Ambleside, West Vancouver, and Jeremy was hired by Rekord Marine, a wholesale marine outlet where he was lead salesman.

CHAPTER 16

Exploring the Alaska Coast
1982–1988

Glacier Bay had been so exciting and impressive that I kept thinking and reading about what the rest of the raw coast might be like between Prince William Sound, Icy Bay (uninhabited), Yakutat Bay, Lituya Bay (uninhabited) and the popular Glacier Bay. Looking at a chart, I calculated the whole trip from Vancouver and back would take ten weeks, but I only had three weeks' holiday. How to achieve this? Was it safe to go? Reading the Alaska Pilot which, like all "Pilots," gives marine and weather conditions in areas where you might wish to sail, provided the following, which is enough to scare the pants off anybody:

The Aleutian Low looms over the North Pacific as a climatic warning to mariners navigating the Alaskan waters. This semi-permanent feature is made up of the day-to-day storms that traverse these seas in a seemingly endless procession.

And with these storms come the rain, sleet, snow, the howling winds and the mountainous seas that make the northern Gulf of Alaska and the southern Bering Sea among the most treacherous winter waters in the Northern Hemisphere.

Sustained winds may reach 60 to 70 knots …

Extreme wave heights of 60 to 75 feet …

Luckily for us, this exceptional weather occurs in the winter, and we knew from our earlier experience of sailing up from Hawaii that the weather was likely quite moderate.

Thus, in late 1982, I drew up a plan with the whole schedule and costs for ten weeks where my boat would make the trip, but three separate groups would sail it. This "do it now" plan was put to friends, and after much discussion, three crews were found by April 1983. The leader of each group had the same type of boat, had previously sailed offshore, and all were friends, which made discussions easier. My boat, *Sky One Hundred*, was not used but Dr. Peter Padwick took his boat, *Justa,* in July, and sailed to Valdez in two weeks where his crew left him. Heather, two young guys, Mark Webber and Rob Barr, and I flew up to Valdez. We joined Peter for the three-week trip along the coast to Glacier Bay and Juneau, the area Heather and I planned to see. I never did tell Heather the month we were going was the only month in the year when it had not snowed.

In fact, the weather was fine and we had blue skies and fair winds most of the time. In Prince William Sound, at 4 a.m. on the second morning, we had a shock when we felt *Justa* jolting and vibrating with a kind of roaring noise and realized it was an earthquake. It was later determined as 6.4. We were pleased it had not been the massive 9.2 mega earthquake of 19 years earlier which caused vertical up and down land movements of up to 30 ft and the 60 ft lateral movement of a small island in the Sound. We found the hundred-mile-wide Sound was packed with thirty main glaciers, some rising like highways disappearing up into cloud-covered mountain tops. I commented in my book when we just drifted having supper surrounded by glaciers: *"The stillness created no sound except for the low murmur of our voices issuing forth more adjectives describing the magical scene of complete isolation in the descending coldness. It was in fact, 13 July, and a 26th anniversary dinner for Heather and myself, one we will not easily forget."*

Our 21st anniversary had occurred when sailing up to Glacier Bay in 1978. Erica had made us what we called a swimming-pool cake, deep at one end, shallow at the other, caused by the fluid mix and the heel of *Sky One Hundred* from not having a gimballed stove.

After a rough eastward sail, the entrance to the uninhabited Icy Bay, our second stop, was so overwhelming with the surrounding mountains including Mount Saint Elias, 18,150 ft that a kind of madness descended on the crew with some of them, including Heather, leaping into the surf declaring it warmer than English Bay. Next day we sailed to the back of the bay past where the glacier terminal face had been only seventy years ago.

Sailing a hundred miles further along the coast, we entered Yakutat Bay as night was falling and responded to a MAYDAY, MAYDAY, radio call for help from a small power boat. Peter later received a splendid letter from the rear admiral of the US Coast Guard, Juneau, thanking him for the assistance which was in the *"highest traditions of the sea..."* Next day in the Yakutat village, we learnt that only four sailboats had visited there that year. We sailed 35 miles north into the bay and explored the five-mile face of Hubbard Glacier, the biggest in North America, leaving for an overnight sail to Lituya Bay about 8 p.m.

Our excitement was extreme, sailing along this virtually raw and isolated coast as dawn broke the next day. Later we carefully entered the narrow entrance of the T-shaped Lituya Bay and anchored. This bay had recorded the highest wave in the world, 1,720 ft, higher than the Eiffel Tower, caused by a 7.2 earthquake along the Fairweather fault line at the head of the bay. It occurred in 1958, BC's Centennial year, when the BC climbing team had just climbed Mount Fairweather and had luckily been flown out just two hours and ten minutes before the earthquake, which caused a 100 ft wave to pass over their campsite, where they had been celebrating.

As we cruised on towards the popular Glacier Bay, swapping chores and jokes, we could not but reflect how the earlier explorers Bering, Cook, Vancouver and La Perouse in the 1700s found and reacted to this coast. At that stage in the Little Ice Age, glaciers might still have been almost out to the coastline. This might have caused a more or less continuous line of ice with few places to seek shelter and drop anchor.

In Juneau, we met up with Charles Priester and his crew, including our friend, Ernie Pennick, the third group, and had a fun exchange of news and experiences over some snooker games in a local pub. We left them to take over the boat and bring it home while Peter and our crew flew home. This rare, adventurous and successful trip, almost before the steady run of cruise ships headed up there, is described in my book, *Explore the Alaskan*

Coast, which had a nice review by the *Pacific Yachting* magazine ("the account of Patrick and Heather Hill's Alaska explorations will have many skippers longing for this *last frontier*"), and a five-star rating by Amazon. It was reviewed by Robert Graf, the first Canadian to sail single-handed through the Northwest Passage (2015) without outside assistance. This is such an attractive area that over 900,000 cruise passengers head there each year from Vancouver, but I am saddened that our two friends Peter and Charles have since passed away to other seas.

Before we took off for this Alaskan trip, Heather and I were pleased to see Erica graduate from Carson Graham Senior School and start work at the West Vancouver SPCA. She loved animals and was always at ease around them. She also did a number of house-sitting jobs, baby sitting and sometimes looked after a boy who was older than her and whose parents were away — an odd situation. Then, worryingly to Heather and me she bought a 250cc Yamaha motor bike. We also worried about one of her boyfriends.

In 1986, Vancouver held a World's Fair of Transportation and Communication, a marvellous five-month party with magnificent buildings and a show called EXPO 86. Heather and I went every evening when free and were particularly pleased that Erica had got herself a full-time job as an EXPO attendant dealing with and controlling visitors.

After EXPO, she worked on a ranch and then at Swan Wooster Sandwell (SWS) for a year. (Swan Wooster Engineering had been bought out by Sandwell). She used to tell me the low-down of what was going on with people in the company. I think though, a desire had been developing in Erica for change of scenery and travel, and she finally left for the UK. We were proud of her ability to take off and find her feet there with a place to live, a job and dealing with all the necessities of settling in a new environment. We were sorry she never came back. In the following summer, 1990, she travelled around Europe for five weeks suffering a lot of unwanted hassle; she really enjoyed the following three weeks when Jeremy joined her. A year later she met Leo, her husband-to-be, and they were married on 13 June 1998. They are now in their second house with two children Ellen, born 1999 and Kira born 2002. Erica and Leo both have their own businesses as a computer and IT specialist and an accountant, respectively. We are in regular touch. Skype is a wonderful app, and we have a good, friendly relationship with them and with Jeremy and his family. We are very thankful for this.

CHAPTER 17

The Other Family
2004 onward

In 1964, after Heather and I had left Edmonton and returned to live in Vancouver, I started learning Spanish because I wanted to be able to work in South America. Although my British passport was still valid, I thought it was time to apply for a Canadian passport. Part of the paperwork required by the authorities was to provide documentation of my English parents. As my father had died when I was fourteen, I wrote to my mum for the required documentation. It was a surprise when, about three weeks later, I received a letter from my eldest brother, Michael telling me our parents had never married. He advised me in pleasant terms that the four of us, of course, were bastards. It was not a normal kind of letter, and I might have been shocked but was not. Twenty or forty years earlier, you might have been shocked, but I guess I am a kind of free spirit and had no negative reaction, certainly not against my parents. I realised it was a forewarning in case I read the documentation and suddenly saw that our parents had never been married. With my particular concerns of the time, the news did not worry me at all; in fact, I found it rather amusing. It certainly did not affect my getting a Canadian passport.

However, getting our citizenship involved a chancy incident. Heather had an appointment early in the morning with a judge when she swore her oath to Canada. I went later to the same judge, swore my oath, and the judge said, "That will be $10." With shock, I explained I had no money as I thought my wife had paid for me in the morning. The judge then advised, in severe terms, there were over 200,000 applicants for citizenship, and I had better hustle on down to the bank, get the money and be back within thirty minutes or it would be too late. Did I ever hurry!

Many years later in 2004, when our children had their own families, something completely different surfaced. On a summer visit to the UK, Heather and I had been to see Tony, my next brother up, and his wife, Ann, who lived in Hailsham. Tony had always been a collector, maybe a bargain hunter, and his garage was so full of items that he kept their car out on the street. He loved producing things that he was proud of having bought. Some of the musical instruments were really impressive, but on this occasion, he gave me an envelope saying it might be of interest. Carefully opening it, I was amused to be reminded that I was still a bastard, but this time I learnt a lot more. It was a copy of a four-page letter, sent twenty years earlier and 38 years after our father died, to Michael from a lady in Hertfordshire who suggested we were related to her family. I've typed out the key parts of the letter.

Hertfordshire
30 Aug 1984
Dear "Uncle Mike,"

Sorry to have taken so long to write. When I phoned you, I was really expecting to eliminate your father from my researches, rather than find a whole new set of relations! It might otherwise have done to sort out the bits that will interest you, because I am in the early stages of a pregnancy, and therefore very tired. The usual 2-3 free hours in the evening after a day with my exhausting son are therefore spent in a comatose slump rather than a useful activity.

Anyway, I enclose the outline of my researches to date, plus what I know of your father's first family.

My mum, Peggy, is unfortunately permanently resident in hospital: she is suffering from Alzheimer's disease, or senile dementia, so would not comprehend if we told her of your existence. In any case, as the eldest, she had a clear memory of her father, but never spoke of him — presumably trying to forget what must have been a pretty unhappy home life towards the end.

My mum and Jennie never got on very well and have not been in direct touch for many years. I presumably met her when I was small, but have no recollection of her at all, and the information about her comes from Pamela. My father recently established contact with her (Jennie) because of mum's illness; she lives not all that far from you, in Hampstead Garden suburb.

Pamela married a Canadian in the war, went to Canada with him and chose to stay there after the divorce. She lives in Regina, Sask., and I think her daughter Laura and family are quite near; Linda has moved west to Vancouver. After I spoke to you I did manage to write Pamela a brief note – she was fascinated! She had always understood, as we had, that her parents did not separate until about 1925, so how much her mum knew or suspected in the meantime is anybody's guess. She (Pamela) hopes to visit England in the spring, incidentally.

My father retired three years ago after being a Reader in Greek Literature at the University of Oxford. My brother teaches maths at Clifton College, Bristol. I am married to a barrister, a Hill from Somerset. I retired to have Richard after working in the British Library in the British Museum.

I don't know much more to flush out the bare bones of the "ancestor" tree. I hope that you will be able to give me some details about your father and grandfather – I have the outline of your grandfather's career from his obituary in the Times and a few bits and pieces about your father's early career, but not much more. Any reminisces would be appreciated. And would you by any chance have photographs of either of them that I could get copied?

So there we are! I look forward to seeing you/meeting you. I always felt deprived in childhood, having no aunts or cousins except ones we never heard from, and no uncles at all. Now at last...you must let us know how many cousins I have got!

For the moment, farewell,
Your niece, Gillian

My first reaction was, what is this about? Your father's first family? I looked at Tony with a "What the heck?" look. Tony said, "Yes, he was married and had three daughters, Peggy, Jennie and Pamela." This was a staggering piece of news that we discussed for a while, as we learnt that he did not marry my mum because he could not get a divorce from his wife. I was so surprised by this news that I never did ask Tony how long he had known this. When we got back to Erica's house, she read the letter and immediately said, "I'll find out if she still lives at this address." She did, and via a phone call, we told her who we were and arranged to meet Gillian at her house.

It was a strange kind of meeting, with a certain level of restraint when we met her and her daughter, Alison, in their nice house. This eased fairly quickly when she showed us the family tree she was working on. Over a traditional cup of tea and a sandwich, we heard her story. She was the youngest daughter of Peggy. After an interesting chat, I agreed, when we arrived back in Canada, to send her whatever photos and data we had to add to her collection. It was a relatively warm meeting but I, frankly, was not particularly keen to spend time on pursuing my background as I felt there were too many other things to do in life.

The key issue that struck between the eyes, was that our mum was pregnant with Michael at around the same time as our father's legal wife was pregnant with the youngest of the three daughters; in fact, Michael was born 8 May 1921 and Pamela on 10 January 1921, just four months apart. Now we did start thinking about my father along with a number of questionable "do it now" jokes. Was he some kind of hot rod? Did we have any other family around? When reviewing addresses, it turned out that everybody lived in approximately the same area. Did our father have a fast bicycle, or did he just run fast? While Michael knew, when did Tony or Ray know? Anyway, I was not interested in following up the trail and, after a couple of letters, our communication would likely have faded. But not yet, as on return, we found a message on our phone from a Linda Medland living in Vancouver, saying that she was the daughter of Pamela and that we were likely related because of my English accent. That made Heather and I laugh. Obviously, there had been some fast communication while we were in the UK. Linda's mum Pamela, the youngest daughter, had married a Canadian in 1944 and emigrated to Regina after the war. This was yet another surprise, as Michael's son, Michael, was living there when Linda contacted us.

At the earliest opportunity, we invited Linda to our home, along with Jeremy, our son, and Ramy, his wife. Linda turned out to be a likeable person and, as we swapped question and answer, a huge surprise surfaced — one that proved to have an incredibly tenuous connection that brought forth many jokes and much laughter. It turned out that Linda had taught music at Jeremy and Erica's Carson Graham school! This was difficult to accept but was proved when Jeremy went and produced his school yearbooks. On searching through the pictures, there Linda was in one of the group pictures. We have experienced many incredible coincidences, but this seemed to be an extraordinary one. I imagine some talented mathematician, maybe Gillian's brother, could calculate the chances of this happening. Later in the conversation, a further connection arose, which made us all laugh and wonder what was coming next in this afternoon of revelations, when Ramy, on hearing Linda's surname, said, "You live at such and such road, in fact, at number 2345." We all looked at her in surprise, and Linda asked, "How do you know that?" Ramy replied, "I was a postie in that area and I remember all the names and addresses." Gob-smacked, yes!

These revelations might be called the family skeleton, but I have heard of skeletons in so many families that I have thought of advertising for families to advise me about their skeletons.

Later, Pamela came to Vancouver for a visit, and we were pleased to meet such a pleasant person, along with Linda. Pamela passed away two years later.

Because I am writing my memoir, I have naturally contacted Linda again and have also been in touch with Simon Bird, who was adopted by the middle daughter, Jennie. He has also been making a family tree and has a big write-up on my father on the internet. Tony's daughter, Deborah, continues researching our family's background. I have always said when she finds a past contact surfacing with a nice castle and some 300 acres of land, to let me know. She hasn't found that yet, but on our visit to UK in 2017, told me she had traced my mum's side back to Elizabeth Godolphin (1681–1756). The Godolphins were well-established and a big name in Cornwall owning some nineteen tin and copper mines. Surprisingly, Deborah had visited some of the old mine sites out of interest, and the internet advises that the whole area is a UNESCO World Heritage site. I'm sure she will continue her research, and I note that Jonah Jenkin Milford (1815–1898) was part of the family tree and perhaps the reason for the Milford in my name and Jeremy's. At the time of writing this I had just picked up a Poldark book from our library and was excited to read the Godolphin name in the first couple of pages. I wonder if our researchers will find any more contacts to stir our imagination.

Circular Quay seen from Kiribilli, Sydney

Huge waves heard pounding on the rocks at night.

Nine span Bethanga Bridge Project

Duck-bill platypus and a possum

My site shed.
∨
∨
∨

Black slide area caused
workers to run.

Walk up slope.

Tried to drive up.
No Luck

Real steep going
down a 1000ft.

Ayers Rock in Red Center

"Get away, yer black sods, get away."

In three hours rain flooded to top of pos

Heather + parrots   Proud abo   Jeremy + flie

A three trailer load passing
Devils Marbles

Thorny devil dragon

Wild camels now
used for tourist trips

A rough drive down
river bed to go for
a swim

On Barrier Reef
boating out from
Proserpine

On dirt track
heading for the
coast

Blankensteins
see us off from
Melbourne

Tutankhamum Mask

Back of King's seat

Why the suit?

Back in England

Our first home in
Brantwood with
balcony we built

Arches I built after
first trip to Per

The Davison's
Whistler ski
cabin called the
'Stagger Inn'

Ted, Gloria,
Jamie, Norman,
Heather, Patsy

Massive storage sheds at bulk terminal, Port Moody

Westshore Bulk Terminal B.C. 22 mtpy coal

Richards Bay Bulk Terminal S.Af. 60 mtpy coal

'Rich' Taj Mahal built
in the 17th century

Poor lady loading coal by
hand into rail cars

Me sleeping in
Nehru's bed in his
summer home,
Paradeep

Snake charmer holds cobra up
for tourists as he plays his flute

A super quick photo as just blasted
upwards when flying too low over a
smoking volcano in Chile

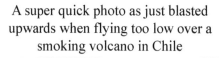

Steward connecting
oxygen tubes for us
in old Dakota plane.
Note freight

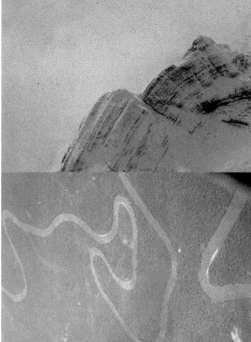

Narrow high
altitude pass
over Andes

Typical river
course with
bow-lakes
nearly formed

Access to Iquitos by Amazon on air. No road

Hauyna Pichu 94oft higher
via Death Stairs

Macchu Picchu 1967

Urubamba River seen from
top of Hauyna Pichu

Leaving Church Lima

Overloaded truck, Pullcalpa.
Note holes in river bank

42ft mold
done after
three months

Ready for
launch after
three years

Sky One Hundred being
towed to Mosquito Creek

Our dream underway
Complete Bliss

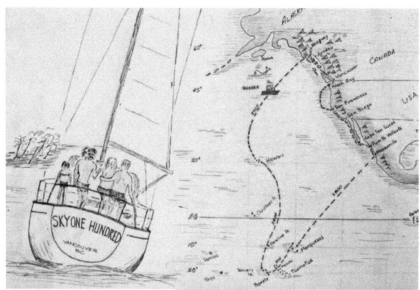

Our Big Family Trip

The Society Islands Bora
Bora on far right

Never mind the 49th wave,
this is the 149th one

Sky One Hundred off
Lamplugh Glacier in
Glacier Bay 1978

An arena built on flat groun

Unusual rocks with caves

Ephesus Library

Goodbye to friends Bev & Dave

Access to arena above

An unusual clock in the Hermitage Museum,
St. Petersburg

Pamukkale tiered calcium terraces   Cappadocia underground quarters

Feluccas on River Nile

Honk Kong, living quarters   Temple in Bangkok

Bangkok, river
taxi speeding on
a klang

ALASKA COAST TRIP

Mt. St. Elisa 18,150 ft.
Icy Bay

Peter at Hubbard
Glacier, biggest
in North America.
Yakutat Bay

Mark, Heather, Peter
aboard Justa

Calving
with seal
resting on
floating
ice floe

Machhapuchhre 21,320 ft

Scary as 300 ft drop

Chaynba left, Gancha right

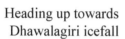

Heading up towards
Dhawalagiri icefall

She made the
best noodle
soup I have
ever had

Powerful vista of New York when sailing the R. Hudson

Last lock of 35 on classic Erie Canal

French Silk Cabin

Smiling Peruvian lady shopping in Cusco

Exploring the warm blue Bahamian waters

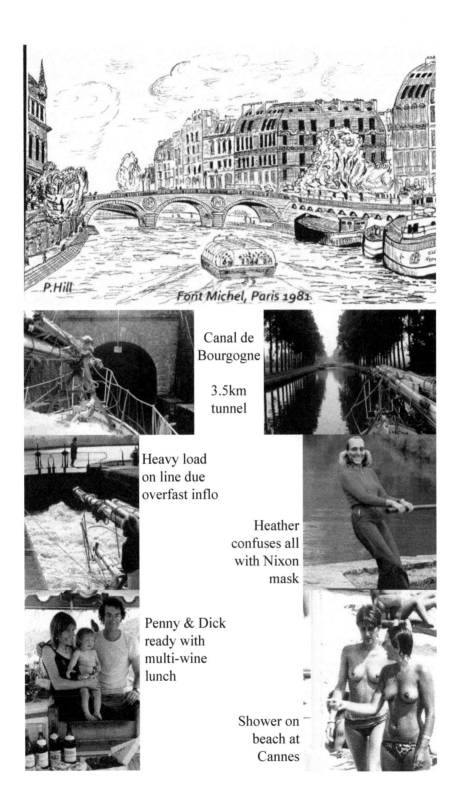

P.Hill

Font Michel, Paris 1981

Canal de Bourgogne

3.5km tunnel

Heavy load on line due overfast inflo

Heather confuses all with Nixon mask

Penny & Dick ready with multi-wine lunch

Shower on beach at Cannes

X marks Sky One Hundred at Straits Race start

Chichen itsa, Mexico

Heather gliding, France

Superb Concorde just landed, London

Roger and Heather in our boat

Olga helps me stand for two minutes after being paralysed for twenty-six days

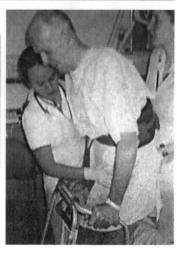

Bahamian Junkanoo Festival

Vancouver family

Parrot takes cash

Mum with UK family

Heather used to smoke

Chaunba & Gancha on Dhawalagiri looking across Kali
Gandaki's huge valley at Annapurana peaks. Larjung at bottom.

Jeremy just sailed from Hawaii & welcomed by Jenni

Family on VOLENDAM trip in Alaska 2015
Leo, Heather, Roger, Erica, Me, Jeremy, Riley, Kira, Ellen

Colwyn Glacier

Route up Mt. Baker, 10,750 ftt.

Colwyn Glacier

Crevasse rescue.

From our balcony early morning sun striking Mt. Baker.
Vancouver harbor in foreground. Mt. Shuksan to right.

SELECTED FAMILY TREE

Elizabeth GODOLPHIN(1681-1756)
7th great-grandmother

William HILL III .... A3see left
b.31.10.1886
d.15.5.1946
m. 28.1.1911
Georgina HASKINS
b.12.3.1888
d.Ag7.1949

J.HIll (baker)   (trimmer) J.SMITH
d.3.4.1881   m.11.5.1844 d.?
b.??
WH 1(shoe maker)   b.?   J.SMITH
d12.11.1932   m.15.1.84   d.17.11.32
b.28.3.1852   b11.7.61
WH 11(journalist)   E.YOUNG
WH III   A3

Jonah Jenkin Milford(1815-1898)

Nora HEWITT
b. 05.1892   m.no

Georgina HILL(Peggy)
b.21.6.1911
m.19.6.1939 Spencer BARRETT

Gillian BARRETT
b.6.10.1947
m.10.9.77 Greg HILL

Jennie HILL
b5.3.1918
m.july.1939 Derek Ross BIRD

Simon Bird b.5.1954
both adopted
Susan Bird b.2.1959

Pamela HILL.C (1)
b.10.1.1921
m.1.3.1944 Monty MEDLAND

Linda MEDLAND.C
b.26.12.1944

Laura MEDLAND C.
b.30.4.1950
m.27.7.1973

(1) immigrated to Canada
& divorced

Michael C.   Michael HILL
b.13.7.59   b. 08.05.1920   d. 01.01.1967
m.12.10.96   m. 1946 Joan
Val.26.5.56   d. 011.1997

Angela   Barry   Raymond HILL
b21.10.79   b.27.1.50   b.01.07.1923
im.2.10.71 m.1944 Lillian d.

Michelle
            Deborah   Richard H   Anthony HILL
            b.25.2.61 b. 1958 A. b.30.05.1925
            m.   m.1951 Audrey d.

Natasha   Jane
b. 20.7.92 d. 01.2018

Barry   Wendy
b.   m. 2017 Anne

Robina
d.

Kira M   Ellen M   Erica   Riley H C.   Jeremy H C. Patrick HILL C.
b.13.3.02   b.2.07.99   b. 21.3.65 b.27.2.98   b.17.7.61   b.08.03.1932
L.Mellett   m 13.6.98   m.28.5.92   m. 13.07.1957
                        Barry   Ramy dv.   Heather
                        Jenni   d.

Note; all live in UK except where name marked .C or .A

Canada .. Australia

CHAPTER 18

Canal de Bourgogne
1982

After returning from our South Seas trip, we received a letter from Paris and wondered who it was. When I slit open the letter, I said to Heather, "Hey, look at this, it's from Dick and Penny who are in Paris, and they want us to help them take their boat through the Canal de Bourgogne to Lyon. Dick has a bad elbow, their baby is a handful, and they still have their parrot." We both laughed at the thought of the parrot. We had sailed with them as buddy boats when we had cruised in the South Seas, and now they were making their way home after three years more sailing.

I immediately thought "Yes," as opportunities like this don't often arrive, and our outlook has always been "do it now." A quick look on the cyberspace highway showed there would be 189 locks over 150 miles and a 3.3 km tunnel connecting the Seine from Paris and the Saone to Lyon. It was an intriguing challenge. A check on my banked time at work indicated I had sufficient time to do this; Heather straightaway said, "Let's go." However, while we had earlier enjoyed their company, living together in a 35 ft boat might not be easy. So we phoned them saying that we'd love to come and help on the condition, which they accepted, that if things did not work out, we would leave, as we wanted to enjoy our holiday, and if they got fed up with us, they should say it is a "no go," and we would leave.

Penny met us off the plane and took us through the Metro to their boat docked on the banks of the Seine. We had a mighty big reunion hearing about their past years of sailing. Two days after visiting Montmartre, the Eiffel Tower, the Louvre and watching wonderful riverboats, we left. That night, when I stepped ashore to tie up, I caught my toe on their top lifeline, two inches higher than ours, and fell awkwardly on the concrete, grazing my knee.

The next night, when docking in a slight drizzle, I was extra careful, but while I stepped across the gap to shore as their boat docked, I did not have enough forward momentum. As I started to fall back towards their boat, I gave a push with my feet to reach the boat so that I did not fall in the water. Unfortunately, as I turned in the air, I fell right on top of a vertical stanchion post with a tremendous whack in my side, gasping as agonising pains surged through me while I hung on to the lifeline with my feet just touching the water.

In desperation, I croaked out, "Dick, Dick, help me, pull me up." He and Heather rushed to help and hauled me up – more agony – and lay me on the foredeck. I thought I would never breathe again, as my body was just jolting in shock. With the rain increasing they slid me along the deck and eased me into the covered cockpit while Penny, fortunately able to speak French, had gone for aid and returned with firemen. As they stomped around and over me, I was scared they would step on me with their large boots. When ready to lift me off, one bent right over me asking if I was okay and I was virtually anesthetised by a solid blast of garlic breath.

At a small local hospital just south of Paris, I was put on a trolley for an X-ray and wheeled along a basement corridor. With lights flashing by overhead, I thought it felt a bit like the old *Dr. Kildare* TV program, but no, suddenly the trolley stopped, and the black guy pushing me started a serious altercation with a white-coated fellow coming the other way. Suddenly, my guy had the other one by the shirt collar and was bashing him against the wall. I closed my eyes, disconnecting from this scene, and found I was being pushed into the X-ray room. Here two operators waved for me to move onto the horizontal X-ray table. It was four inches higher, and neither helped me move despite seeing my laboured efforts.

Finally, I was wheeled back into a room with six beds. Being Sunday, it was packed with visitors. I was told I had four bruised ribs and should stay the night for observation. With my wife and Penny standing by me, all in the open room, a nurse dropped some pajamas on my trolley and started stripping my clothes off. It is amazing how you can suddenly get up from a lying position with painful ribs and undress yourself.

After Heather and Penny left, saying they would see me in the morning, I collapsed back on the bed. There was a roar of conversation from the visitors with many looking in my direction; as each visitor came or left, I'm sure there were four kisses on each cheek and not our normal one or two. While I still quivered in shock from time to time, a passing nurse handed me a thermometer. I was slowly raising it to my mouth, wondering if it was some new type since it seemed unusually large, and not one I had seen before, when the nurse looked back, shrieking, "Non, non, monsieur, a l'intérieur!" pointing to her derriere. I think the visitors got their best laugh of the day from that, as I went through this new exercise and experience.

As the day ended, thank heavens, food was given to patients on trays. My tray was left on the bedside table. As I tried to sit up and reach for it, a visitor took pity, came across helped me sit up, and handed me the tray. I gave him *my full blast of French*, "Merci monsieur, merci beaucoup."

Drifting in and out of sleep during the night trying to find a comfortable position, I decided I would get up early, see the doctor as soon as possible, and leave directly my friends arrived. I was up at 5 a.m. walking up and down, saw the doctor and left after paying 100 francs charge at the gate.

With my lack of usefulness on the boat, caused by pain and shaking when laughing or getting into my bunk, I returned home six weeks later, still in pain. I had another X-ray. The comment was that I had four cracked ribs, and it was lucky I had not burst my spleen. C'est la vie!

Talking to Penny one day, I said, "We have been here nearly three weeks. It's time we were leaving as we are close to Lyon." She said, "No, you have been here five weeks now." I could not believe this, but with the fun we had been having getting their boat through the many locks we helped to operate, taking it through the long narrow tunnel and visiting the villages, vineyards and historic sites, time had just slipped by. In one town, we were reading a plaque dedicated to Canadian soldiers when three locals invited us back to their house and opened up bottles of champagne in thanks for the help Canadian soldiers had given them. It was a humbling moment.

The canal was a complete delight, often tree-lined, running through quaint villages with sweeping views and fields. We moored on the bank wherever we wished to rest for the night or take a walk. People were often fishing and, having watched their efforts, I was convinced that the fish caught were inversely proportional to the size of the long rods. There were few recreational boats and quite a few commercial barges complete with the owner's home and their car. When a big barge came past, the water level would go down, caused by an increase in the water velocity. We had to be careful our keel was not grounded, causing us to slew into the bank or the barge. In the first part of the canal, there was a considerable water flow from early spring run-off. At one point, we went aground and were rather violently pulled free by a tug and barge which ripped a cleat off Dick's boat. Sometimes, as a special and pleasant delight, we would have dinner provided by a lock keeper by the side of their lock, a pleasant and relaxing treat.

We all got on well except for their parrot. He was somewhat territorially minded, and if you put your hand on the hatch when descending into the cabin, it signalled a missile strike which drew blood. After several attacks, I called him the *green bastard*. He could also collect coins off the baccarat board.

In Lyon, after hugs and goodbyes, we drove through the mountains to Cannes, seeing excellent sights on the way. After finding a room and spending a week on the beach complete with topless girls, we took the train back to London.

We later learnt that after all their years of sailing together, Penny and Dick separated. What a shame.

CHAPTER 19

Getting into Real Estate
1980–1985

In early 1961, when we were considering our Australian venture, our friend Norman who worked as an architectural draftsman was wondering where he was going in life. I met Norman after meeting his wife Gloria in my Spanish lessons, and we had been friends for a long time. When Heather and I returned to Vancouver from our two-year stay in Australia and London, we found Norman had left his architectural company, joined up with a colleague and in late 1961, started their own construction business, installing reinforcement in high-rise buildings. This was the start of the high-rise boom, and he finally sold out in 1968. He and Gloria then left on the *Canberra* going to England while I got down to work again. Further, he was making money in the real estate market and kept urging me to invest money in the same direction.

I did once see a house close to ours boast a Sold sign on its 'For Sale' sign and then, a few days later, saw the For Sale was on again. It was the "flip" time, and the agent told me the buyer could not get financing. When he responded that the seller was a Chinese doctor in Hong Kong, I said, "Offer this lower price with no subjects and 48 hours to accept." Suddenly I had a house, but not enough money so I called up Norman, Jamie and an architect friend, Chuck, and we bought it. We, mainly Norman and I, did a lot of cleaning up, painting and re-did the bathroom.

I then set about selling it myself, spending $50 on For Sale signs including one on top of the car. I put them all out on three open house weekends and in came the people.

This was a strange new experience for me. Most viewers were okay, but two ladies came one Sunday afternoon and started sniffing, saying there was an odd smell. I did not want them wandering around saying that but they left in a huff, saying they were going to report me when I said it was not there until they had arrived. Amusing really, because they didn't realize I wasn't an agent. Then an aggressive guy came in demanding the price and when I told him said, "That's ridiculous, no one would pay that." I asked him, "What would you pay then?" and it was so low that I asked him, "Do you watch TV?" With an odd look at me, he said, "Yes," and then I suggested, "Why don't you go home and watch TV as you will never get a house like this at your price." He nearly took the door off its hinges when he left and was going to report me. I wondered who to? We bought it for $95,000 and sold it for $135,000 after three open houses.

Later I left SWE to try this apparently profitable business. I even took a Real Estate course but never used it as an agent. When Norman sold his business, we both joined up to buy and sell property supported by an investors club.

In the first year, the process went well as investors believed the market was on the rise. It was during this time that Heather and I booked the first of two flotilla boat cruises around the islands on the east coast of Greece and Turkey. On the way home, we met up with John Newton of the West Vancouver Yacht Club who had his boat, *Pachena*, at Lymington, south England for the racing. Since the crew had not yet arrived, he allowed us to stay at their quarters if we cooked breakfast and then have a trial race with them the next day. That night when we took him out to dinner, he mentioned that the housing market in Vancouver was beginning to collapse. I felt sick over this news, and on return, found our timing was not the best and probably the worst, as by 1980, within two years, the whole market was slowing down. While we had properties on options-to-buy, these timed out, so we had bought them and were trying to get the properties re-zoned. The situation worsened and finally came the pay-up time.

Our friend, Darryl Delmotte, had earlier advised me to watch the cash flow as it was a controlling feature. This problem caused Heather to go back to work and me to offer my services to SWE.

These were, fortunately, accepted, and I urgently called upon all my friends to get me elected as a dividend shareholder again. This was a great relief, as the engineering market was slowing and key projects were being finished, causing our staff to be reduced from some 550 to 170 people. I think I was next to go. It was a very concerning period, during which the local market had more than 20% of engineers unemployed. I survived though and kept earning money. It took two or three years before we recovered our savings. It had been a really tough time, with monetary restraints, while Norman and Gloria went off to work in London with their friend, Nelson Skalbania, a recognized real estate operator.

Being back at work was a good feeling, but all work we were bidding on had to have reduced profits and sometimes no profit but just enough to pay the overheads and keep remaining staff working.

By 1983, we had now been in our *Brantwood* home for some 20 years and the mortgage had been paid off, but I was beginning to want a better view and a newer place. So I started looking around and asked a broker to let me know when he saw something at my price in the area I wanted. Heather knew what I was doing but being rather attached to our house and area did not really want to move. The broker called after a while and said there was one on *Overstone*, near Gleneagles golf course. I went and saw it, liked it and liked the view. Heather saw it and was partially interested. To convince her of the benefit of the move, I suggested we rent the *Brantwood* house for a year and, if she did not like the *Overstone* house, we could always move back. We could just about manage the money required and so now we had two houses. However, on the second evening in the new house, sitting out on the balcony looking at the view across to Passage Island I asked, "Would you ever think of moving back?" and the quick answer was, "No way." Now the family was spread over a larger, more convenient house and I had to deal with renting our old house with all its problems.

Shortly after we moved into *Overstone*, I noticed my neighbour putting his leaves and old cuttings over the fence into our garden. When I mentioned this to him, he said, "No, you are on my land." I said, "But the fence is here." and he said, "I only built it there for convenience, but the border is further over there." That was another lesson when buying a house – check the boundaries. Later, when I decided to make the living room balcony bigger, I had a surprising but amusing problem. It was supported on one side by the house wall and had two 4 x 4-inch supporting posts on the opposite outer side. I was going to make it three times bigger and had brought the timber to do this. One Saturday, when Heather was out shopping, I thought I would just slightly lift the outer side to see how flexible the balcony was. As I had barely levered the edge up, by standing on the end of a 14 ft plank, used as a lever, I was staggered to see the two posts just fall out. There had been no nail connection at the top. Now I had to wait on the end of the plank until Heather returned to replace my weight, or the balcony would have collapsed. Bill McLachlan came the next day to help.

Some eighteen years passed, during which time my neighbours kindly allowed me to carefully cut their trees so that we maintained our view. When they finally passed away, their house was sold to an Iranian builder. When I asked him what he was going to build, he would not discuss it, and because he was on a corner lot, the footprint of any house he built could be anywhere he liked. This meant we might have no view, so Heather and I decided to sell although she was not too keen after being in the house for so many years.

Now retired, I went searching for a cheaper condo to add more money to our retirement fund. I saw a nice one conveniently located but said to the agent, "This is too expensive for me but when you see one at a lower price, please let me know." About four months later, after we had made offers on other places which, in reflection, thank heavens, had not been accepted, he called and said, "This condo is not listed yet, but the people want to sell." When we walked in late on a Monday evening and saw the huge balcony (58 ft x10 ft) with its international view of Mt. Baker in the distance and across English Bay to Nanaimo, Heather immediately said, "I like it." I said to the agent, "Come first thing tomorrow and we'll write an offer."

The agent came at nine the next day and said, "Sorry, it went late last night." We were both disappointed, especially as when we left, a local lady called out, "Hello Patrick, do you remember me?" "Yes, Erika, you used to be on Bikini Beach thirty years ago." A day later, we found out we knew the couple below in the condo, called John and Margaret Hill; Erika was in the unit above; and the man who owned it, Murray, had painted our boat, and had been a partner with our son Jeremy. This was another event in our lives where we had past connections. John Hill called me on Wednesday and said there were still people looking at the condo above. With a "do it now" impulse, I immediately called Murray and said, "I'll buy your condo for the price you want with no subjects." He said, "Write it up and if the offer falls through, it will be yours." Four days later, our agent said it had fallen through as the other people wanted an inspection. How lucky can one get and, again, what a small world.

We were elated to have this condo but still had to sell our house within three months. Our agent, from whom we got a reduced commission, finally found a buyer with a week to spare, by which time we were in a sweat but had arranged a temporary mortgage. A lady came and said it was just what she was looking for and would take any furniture we did not want. Because she wanted to complete the deal immediately as she was leaving the next day, she with her agent and us with ours ended up at different tables in a Caulfield coffee shop while we negotiated a final price. It was not a normal process but effective.

Later that year, we asked my brother, Raymond and his wife, Lillian if they would like to join us in our new condo. They did, renting an RV, and enjoyed driving through southern BC. They particularly liked sailing with us and Ray even tried out our windsurfer. Tony and Anne had come years earlier to our other house. We asked Michael and offered to pay his fare, but it seemed he was not interested.

In 1984, our sailing friend Sam Sydneysmith (wife Jill), who helped form the Bluewater Cruising Association (BCA) wrote to us. He had got us into BCA while we were cruising in the South Seas. He was an economist working in Malawi for the Canadian International Development Agency and said they were coming to the end of his two-year term. Were we interested in a trip there before they left? We immediately said, "Yes please, and can we bring Erica?" The reply was "Yes," and they started organizing a camping session in the bush. The camping was in a new area, with shelters still being set up. After we had jeeped out to the site, Heather and I found we were to sleep in a small tent. It was no problem because the remoteness in the bush was a delight. Sitting around the campfire at night in the warm air with the clear, starlit sky above while chatting and drinking our nightcaps brought back memories of our sailing days.

After nightcaps on our second night, we loaded on to two jeeps and headed off into the bush. After a while, our guide stopped and listened to the shrieks and chattering of a baboon and said, "I think something's going on." Then we drove towards the sound. We stopped at the bottom of a large tree, where there were four hyenas, and we could hear the crunching of something being eaten above, with the occasional noise of pieces hitting the ground. The guide thought it was likely a baboon being eaten. Sitting on the top of our jeep, we listened to this for about 20 minutes when it finally stopped while the hyenas were still barking. Then the star of the scene, a beautiful spotted leopard, emerged into view in the headlights, slowly pacing down the sloping trunk of the tree. As it stepped onto the ground, the snarling and barking of the hyenas intensified, but with complete disdain, it strolled through them and by our jeep. It was so close, like 20 feet, that I, as a gentleman, eased behind Heather. Later, when telling people about this magnificent evening, some said they had been coming for several years but had never seen a leopard. These good memories will last for a long time.

While with Sam and Jill, we received a fax from Jeremy saying that he and Dennis, his sail-making friend, had taken our latest used boat that I had just purchased, and had won the around

Bowen Island race, four hours ahead of the second boat. I thought "Great!" and sent congratulations, but when I returned, I found the boat had been stripped bare of all non-essential sailing gear to make it lighter and faster. When I skippered it the next year, I got third place. Bah!

CHAPTER 20

Interesting Engineering
1955–1995

Although "interesting engineering" might be an oxymoron for some readers, my forty years as a professional engineer have always been interesting.

Design work was my initial target but I soon found planning projects were of greater interest. I found out the greatest challenge was seeking and bidding for new studies and projects to keep our staff working. Getting to meet a potential client and convincing them of our company's talent and capability to bring their job to a successful conclusion needs, on most occasions, some finely tuned persuasion. As an engineering specialist, I rose to director of projects and the director of business development in Swan Wooster Sandwell (SWS).

The work has taken me on many occasions outside Canada to Chile, Peru, Venezuela, Ecuador, Columbia, Brazil, Indonesia, Australia, South Africa, the USA, UK, Hong Kong, Malaysia, Philippines, Thailand, Pakistan, India, Taiwan and Surinam.

Although I described some projects earlier, I might mention a couple more. One job I had with the Iron Ore Company of Chile was for the port design and building of a major iron ore ship loading system for 250,000 DWT (cargo weight in tonnes) bulk ships in Guacolda, Chile which was a challenging project because the ships were much bigger than we had handled before, there were no tugs to assist in docking the ships, and it was a major earthquake area. Our American client, our marine manager and I first visited Rotterdam and Bantry Bay in Ireland to view operations of ships up to 300,000 DWT. With the design completed, the huge steel piles along with piling gear were delivered to the site, but the job was suddenly delayed for two years.

When it was ready to start again, my American client wanted me to go there with him and, using a four-seater plane, search for some of the piling equipment sent earlier. We once diverted course to have a closer look at a slightly smoking, active volcano. I don't think the pilot had ever taken a physics class because as he chose to fly too low across the vent, the extra hot air blasted us upwards while I managed a quick glimpse of the fires below. I was relieved we still had wings on the plane and could get back on course. We did find all the pile-driving gear that had been dispersed, and the job started.

With piling underway, some rocks were found in the way of one of the two main dolphin piles. I took Stan Cowdell, our marine specialist, with me to help solve the problem. We carefully located the rocks and Stan redesigned the dolphin that was used to protect the ship loader from any damage. We had to stay the weekend but Stan and I drove up into the Andes at around 9,000 ft to have a look at the Portillo ski resort.

At the completion of the design, I had to meet with the client in Tokyo to explain to various Japanese shipping groups over a week how the docking and loading system worked, especially as there were no Chilean tugs available. Arriving late on my first evening in Tokyo, I thought I would go for a beer in the famous entertainment area, Kabukihe. Walking around for a while, I was surprised by the number of drunken businessmen wandering around, some even being carried by their colleagues. When I opened the door to what I thought would be a bar and saw a mass of Japanese men, I just backed out, shutting the door. As I hailed a cab, I felt pleased I had asked the bellboy to write down the name and address of my hotel.

During the meetings, all discussions were in Japanese with translation provided. It was a tiring process but the operation was accepted. When we signed the agreement, an elderly Japanese man who had not said a word during the week said, in perfect English, "Mr. Hill, I would like to frankly discuss this project." I thought to myself, "I bet all these people speak English and now I am in for some trouble." But no, it was a practical discussion and all went well.

On a later site visit during the piling on this project, which was being supervised by Brian Aldous, a sailing friend from Vancouver, an earthquake occurred. At the small hotel where I was sleeping, half the ceiling fell into the room, the sink ripped off the wall, and part of the local church was damaged. Although it was frightening, it was all over in a moment. Engineering trips can be quite different! I was impressed in Chile by the friendliness and humour of the people I worked with and the pisco sours, but oh, they ate so late.

When at SWE, I saw the possibility of bidding on a major study for the Federal Transportation Dept. in Delhi, India, so I made a trip to their office. After waiting in reception, a clerk arrived, picked up my briefcase and led me through various offices which seemed very old and packed with people until I arrived at the head man's office. The study was to examine economic ways, by ships or trains, to take coal out of Bengal Bihar, north of Calcutta and distribute it to coal power plants around the coast of India. My proposal for $350,000 in 1965 won out over international competition, especially a key Dutch company. Bill McLachlan, along with a specialist from Canadian Pacific Railway, travelled with me through the country for some five weeks, gathering data.

Indians were friendly but I was often overwhelmed by the squalor, poverty and dirt, so distinct from our stays in the immaculate top hotels. Wherever there was a blank wall on a sidewalk, people lived there, and in Calcutta, families lived on traffic islands leading to the Howrah Bridge, over the Hooghly River. In Bengal, people loaded coal by hand into rail trucks either by carrying a large single lump on their head or a basket load of smaller lumps and walking up a plank into the rail car. They were mostly barefooted and lived in humpies (crude shelters) by the coal piles. The study was financed by India, so we had to travel by Air India. It was all right to fly into India as they were sometimes not full, but never out, because the toilets became unusable due to the passenger numbers and were often not flushed. I would ask to use first class because of the mess. I managed to visit the Taj Mahal which was the epitome of richness, although crude local workshops used children in near darkness, grinding stones for tourist trinkets.

It was a complex study. We were mainly meeting CEOs and executives at certain ports around India, discussing their plans, schedules and collecting data. At some meetings, there were so many officials present that we called them 20- or 50-foot meetings, depending on the length of the table required. The World Bank kept wanting to add their advice on how to solve the problem. Our report was still being referred to five years later. At the job conclusion, my client did mention that some of his children were being educated in Holland, obviously suggesting a way to get the next job. We met the chairman of each port to discuss the project, but my ultimate contact with the high and mighty was to sleep in Nehru's (former president of India) bed (he wasn't there) at his summer cottage in Paradeep, south of Calcutta. The Paradeep authorities had made lavish preparations for our visit. I now read that the city has the coal import facility they wanted.

Most of my work was the planning, design, building and project managing for bulk handling of coal export terminals. Here, coal arrived by trains from mines, was put into storage piles and then loaded into ships for export. The key equipment used was a car dumper which could rotate rail cars upside down to put the coal onto conveyor belts so it could be stacked in piles according to its grade. The coal was then reclaimed by large bucket wheel reclaimers and loaded onto the ships with a special ship loader.

At SWS, I was given the task of leading a team to bid on a design-build bulk terminal expansion for 60 million tons a year in Richards Bay, South Africa. We were bidding against Soros Engineering of New York and a Dutch company. I first went separately to discuss the project with the RBCT client. Later, I went with our president, a control specialist, and Bill McLachlan, who had travelled around India with me and worked on the Westshore Terminal and the Gualcolda, Chile jobs. In the presentation, ten coal mining companies were represented and it was a nervous time for me to procure this valuable project. When we broke for lunch, the client did not invite me to join him, and I felt I had not been at my best. It was a lonely moment. Nevertheless, we did get the job, and I returned later with Bill to put together a design-build team of South African and Canadian groups for the $300 million, three-year project. When we rejected some local companies, earlier selected by SWS, from our design team, there was a level of ill-feeling. After being awarded the job, subject to our detailed plan being accepted, Bill and I first met the South African rail project co-ordinator in his huge office. Interestingly his opening remark was: "You know, we don't really need help from Americans" implying they could do it themselves. He realised he had just blown it when I said, "You know, as Canadians, we agree."

On many projects, particularly in South America, security for your staff or yourself was necessary. Several incidents occurred. When on a major study in northern Venezuela for Shell Coal International, London, we learnt locals might steal their new 4-wheel drive cars, drive them over the border to Colombia and then call up the owners and negotiate a price to get them back.

On a field trip in an isolated area for the same project, we had an armed guard in case of trouble from local groups. Once when getting off a plane in South America, I saw a table full of labelled guns and knives that had apparently been collected from the passengers, of which I was one. On another flight, I was trying to tell, in my inadequate Spanish, the passenger next to me that crossing a street in Lima was like playing Russian roulette. Not understanding, I drew a picture of a revolver with one bullet in the chamber, and with quick, "Ah, si," he pulled a revolver out of his inner jacket — not your normal fellow passenger.

The most security required was for a major American coal company on a project study I obtained in Colombia. This was another coal project to mine coal and ship it out from Santa Marta, north of Cartagena. When we sent four rail experts to make a first field inspection trip of the railway, the company supplied four, armed local security men to stay with each of our people all the time. That was a warning of what might be needed, especially when I had seen one man carrying a briefcase, walking though the Bogota airport escorted and boxed in by six security men each carrying a vertically raised pump gun on their shoulders. I wondered if he was an important minister or a key drug boss. When bidding on the job, I checked out whether to use Colombian or Floridian security sources.

On visiting Bogota for this project, I never wore a smart suit or carried a briefcase but always dressed down. I never got into an elevator with one or two men in it. Once, when visiting the company's office in Bogota, I had entered an empty elevator, and on turning round, found three men had entered and had their backs to me. Instead of reaching to press the 8th floor, I pressed 2nd, got out at the next floor, and took the next lift to the floor I wanted. When I got out, there were the three guys – one my client, and the other two, his security men. We had a laugh when I told my client I had not recognized him from behind. A Canadian trade official escorted me around for a while, warning me never to go out at night alone. I only stayed at Colombia hotels. The Hilton Hotel was bombed four weeks after I left town. A recent article on the internet indicated: "In the last decade more than 1,500 union officials have been killed in Colombia."

On other occasions, I was inspecting damage or finding out reasons for a failure in areas where extra care was needed, including sticking to the safety rules. Too many workers have fallen from a height by not taking the right precautions.

Sometimes the work seemed dangerous but not nearly as dangerous as the present Heather bought me for my 60th birthday. We were at the Whistler ski resort where we skied a lot as we had two long-term friends there who each owned a cabin, Patsy and Jamie Davidson and Norman and Gloria Elliott. We were always kindly welcomed to share a weekend with them. This weekend, I had been admiring the para-skiers who were floating down from way up the mountain and landing on their skis, and now Heather had bought me a lesson.

On a calm day, a few of us turned up in a small room and were instructed how to put the chute harness on, which cords to pull to go whichever way, and how we would float down a chosen valley. With the hour of instruction over, we each picked up our chutes, took a chair lift up the mountain and then skied across to a steepish avalanche slope. The four of us laid out our chutes behind us, went forward on the slope, put our skis on and attached the harness which was then checked as okay by the expert. She told me, "When I say go, start off down the slope holding onto these two lines, and once you leave the ground don't keep pulling them or else the chute will collapse in front of you. You see the man down there − that is where you will land (it looked like a mile away). He has a red marker in each hand, and when a hand goes down you pull on that cord and you will gently turn in that direction, so follow his directions and you will land where you are supposed to." Then she moved to one side and said, "Go." I had had the back of my skis jammed in the snow, and as I started sliding forward, I felt the pull of the chute rising up behind me, eased my pull on the two cords and next thing I was leaving the ground below and rapidly reached about 200 ft.

"Shoot," I thought, "this no time to panic," especially as I was drifting across the valley. A quick look at the man below showed me one hand was down, so I pulled on that cord, and slowly eased towards him.

With a couple more adjustments, I heard the wind whistling past and saw the ground coming up towards me or rather I was descending onto the level snow base, but in the flat light found I was not sure how far I was off the ground. At the last moment, I got my skis in line with my travel, hit the ground, collapsed the chute and fell over, out of balance. The instructor said, "Pack your chute, ski down and come up again to the same place for a second run."

As I did it a second time, I was able to look around more and at skiers below me. I met Heather at the bottom of the chairlift, and she said, "You have time for one more ride." Was she trying to get rid of me? I thought, because I was already done in. I had a third run from higher up, and I got a couple of shocks — one as I passed over a big change in land formation, causing an unexpected bump in the flight path which made me wonder if all was okay with my harness. Then I was heading across the valley again getting rather close to a rock face and had to pull extra hard on the cord to pull away toward the instructor below to land in front of him.

Well, it was double gin and tonics that happy hour. It was a marvellous thrill but have I got the nerve to go from high up and down into the Whistler Village? I'll think about it.

CHAPTER 21

Retirement
1995 onwards

I retired in late 1995 at the age of 62. I might have gone on working until I was 65, ending up with a nice farewell lunch and a present. This did not happen as, prior to 1995, two directors in my international engineering company, SWS, had been laid off in a procedure of the day that could only be considered insensitive, perhaps cold-blooded. Each director, even one having just returned from lunch, had been separately called into the manager's office. There, each was advised that his service was no longer required and he was handed a letter of dismissal.

The shock of such an experience cannot be readily conceived. The sudden humiliation of being kicked out after many years of responsible service and this, followed by the realisation that your standard of living would likely decline without pay for a while, was not good for your ego. Being escorted back to their offices by an outside impersonal management official, allowed a few minutes to pick up their personal gear, then escorted to the front door without any time for discussion or explanation with their fellow colleagues, all added to their humiliation. Any victim of this process can and often does suffer anger if not depression for a long time afterwards.

I did not wish to experience even the possibility of this process. So, following discussion with a good friend, we decided on a plan by which I could leave in a better social and financial manner. Thus, after some negotiation with the CEO, an arrangement was made which was mutually acceptable to management and myself regarding the monetary and departure terms of my retirement package. One clause in the agreement was that I would not compete in the same market for a period of ten months. This did not concern me as I was quite happy to sit back, rest a while, and explore other aspects of life. Although I enjoyed my challenging work, this break suited me fine.

One of the simple things I always wanted to do on my first day of real freedom was to go down to a local coffee shop, order a coffee, read the daily paper, and watch people and boats active in the harbour — always interesting. I could never understand why some senior retired engineers, even VPs, would come back to the office looking to work again and asking me if there were any jobs or studies they could do. *Didn't they have other interests?* Who wants to be a re-tread working on a junior's salary, as I had heard about in Australia?

Of course, long-term planning of my retirement with Heather started by considering what we would like to pursue. As avid sailors, travel with adventure was always in our mind as was the desire to keep playing tennis and golf.

CHAPTER 22

Consulting in Thailand
1997–98

During my retirement, Heather and I had been thinking about sailing offshore again in "do it soon" terms but towards the end of the ten-month term, a previous client in the shipping business contacted me to ask if I had really retired or was I interested in consulting on a project in Thailand. This sounded like an interesting proposition, especially as I had worked there before, and it would certainly help to increase our retirement kitty. After discussing it with Heather, my acceptance resulted in working not for my past client but directly for Banpu, a major Thai mining company for nearly a year, planning a new local coal import and distribution facility to replace their existing system. Although I needed to work for some periods in Thailand, I would be working mainly from home so our long-term sailing dream could be continued.

On the first of several extended visits to Bangkok, my Thai client met me at the airport and I was pleased to see tennis rackets in his car as he drove me to my hotel. I often carried my racket on trips which provided relaxation and the opportunity to meet other people. Thus, after a hard week's work, Friday nights would be one of relaxation as we battled away at tennis on top of a building at a club, and then went for dinner — a civilised way of life. He took me to many different eating places ranging from restaurants to street vendors. The food was always excellent and my palate experienced flavours so different from our western dishes. Noodles, fried rice and curries with mixtures of pork, chicken, fish, mango and soy sauces were so tasty, but I still think the nasi goring dishes of Indonesia were my favourites.

Also unusual was the experience at the club, as changing and showering seemed a somewhat discreet affair; shower cubicles were separated with a door and there seemed to be no walking around naked. Once when we played at his club, which had a huge swimming pool and even a course for horse racing, he told me he could invite a foreigner but would have difficulty bringing in a local Thai. This seemed strange but the Thai culture came across strong in friendliness, maintaining a pleasant attitude, generally one of smiles.

I certainly enjoyed working with the friendly and helpful Thai office staff. The project work was satisfying and posed a different challenge as I worked on my own. I did find that while the outdoor temperature was warm and humid, the air conditioning in my office was deadly cold — this always seems to be the way in the tropics, especially in restaurants. The staff agreed it was cold, but nothing was done to improve the situation. I would try to block off or re-direct the vent over my office desk so I was not under a freezing down-draft. Sometimes, I left the office and warmed myself in the heat coming up the stairwell. I even tried sitting on my ASUS laptop transformer to keep warm but did not wish to have my bum branded "ASUS."

On my walks to work, it was fascinating to see so many vendors serving foods among the mishmash of buildings among which I noticed a two-column building that looked a bit out of place. It was disconcerting, on occasions, to have a motorcycle on the sidewalk coming up behind at any time trying to pass me. Speed seemed an essential ingredient in the streets, and particularly down the narrow waterways or *klongs* where I could watch long narrow open *long-tail* taxi boats zipping along at 20 knots (40 kph) with their open motors roaring away. Frequently, I would see petite, well-dressed ladies in high heels standing on the narrow edge of a boat or gunwale, who would quickly step off at their destination dock while other passengers boarded the boat as it barely stopped. Crossing a main road required special care because when the lights went green, a mass of motorcycles that had wriggled their way to the front of the cars, would accelerate en masse like a racing start, and zoom directly towards you. Will

Vancouver's traffic be like this in the future?

Towards the end of my stay, my client's contracting partner invited me to dinner, which I thought was a nice, friendly gesture. I met him and his friend at a restaurant and was treated to a delightful local meal. As we finished, he said we would go for a coffee. I thought surely it was not the custom to invite me to his home. No, it was not, but when we strolled along the street, it was to the building with the two columns that I had wondered about when going to work. As we walked up the steps, now covered in red carpeting, the doors opened and we were greeted and surrounded by a swarm of smiling girls all dressed in white.

Oh! I thought, this is going to be a long but interesting evening, and so it proved to be. This seemed to be a regular occurrence with my host as we were herded away in a most delicate fashion, with much giggling, to one of many cozy partially partitioned open areas overlooking a dance floor. As we sat down on a semicircular couch, we were each snug between two girls. Judging by the conversation and body language, I was now sure my hosts had met these girls before. I was provided with one who could speak a smidgeon of English. Actually, a smidgeon of English in Thai only eased the evening slightly.

Among other things, including jokes, much laughter and giggling, we were encouraged to try dishes and drinks of various sorts. I suspected this was some peripheral foreplay to a more private setting; in fact, as the evening progressed there was little doubt, judging by activities I had seen across the floor. After an entertaining period and far too many whiskies, I felt I had done my cultural duty to my hosts. I rose while I still could, thanked them profusely for the evening and, escorted to the door by "my" girls, returned to the streets to wend my somewhat swaying gait back to my hotel.

Towards the end of the year, I was starting to question why I was working again at 64 and not active in the retirement mode. At the same time, I was beginning to think that the proposed project was not going to be economical and, when asked what I thought by the CEO, I carefully suggested one had to be something of a visionary to proceed. On my departure, I was thanked profusely for my help and presented with a number of gifts.

CHAPTER 23

Sailing Wisconsin to
the Bahamas
1998–1999

I had not been home long from Thailand when a kind of restlessness erupted, and after I discussed it with Heather, it seemed she had the same feelings. Although we were both enjoying our daily life, we felt we wanted a new challenge. We figured we could get this with sailing and thought we would go sailing in the Caribbean for a couple of years after buying a boat in Florida. So, we bought tickets to Florida and looked for a boat. We did not find what we wanted there but when sitting in our broker's office, he said, "Here's one in Bayfield." I say sitting, but I was slowly sinking down in his decrepit cane chair. Bayfield marina turned out to be at the west end of Lake Superior. The sailboat was a Beneteau 35s5, five years old with only fifty hours on the motor. Heather and I considered the change of our original plan to one of sailing across the USA and agreed it would be perhaps more challenging than sailing offshore.

We asked Jeremy and Ramy, now living in Toronto, to come and join us to inspect the boat called *French Silk*. I wanted Jeremy's view of it as his would be less emotional than mine. We liked it and bought it in July 1997, came home, and within sixty days had our existing boat for sale, leased the house for a year with mutual agreement for two years, sold our cars, got insurance, organized our finances, packed our things, and were back on *French Silk* ready to go. This was our "do it soon, do it now" philosophy.

After two weeks of getting the boat ready, we left the marina in high spirits and after a smooth seven knot sail, stopped at the Apostle Islands. We were not too happy being woken in the moonlit night in a small isolated bay off one of the islands at nearly midnight. It was a young girl from the harbour patrol asking, "Why is your anchor light not on?" I said, "I am not sure why it is not working, but we have just bought the boat, are on a trial sail, and why does it matter as this bay is completely deserted?"

My comments were not found acceptable; she wanted identification and explained, in detail, the purpose of an anchor light. "Have you not got an emergency anchor light?" It did not seem wise to mention our years of sailing experience, so on answering, "No," we were given a temporary anchor light in exchange for my driver's license which I could get back when I returned the light the following day to their office. I said, "Thank you," thinking she would motor or buzz off and leave us in peace, but no, I had to rig the bloody thing up there and then, to her satisfaction. *"Don't these people have anything else to do in the middle of the night?"*

By mid-November, we were in Miami and were heading out to the Bahamas. We had crossed the Great Lakes to Buffalo, (dropping 21 ft in the massive Sault Ste. Marie locks) and had transited the 380-mile Erie Canal while dropping a further 580 ft through its 35 locks to the Hudson River. After two weeks in New York, we cruised down the 1,080-mile Intra Coastal Waterway to Miami, and out into the blue sea Bahamas.

We aimed to be in the Grand Bahamas for Christmas as we wanted to meet our sailing friends Brian and Maggie Aldous (Brian had worked on the Chile job with me) who were towing their trimaran down there for a holiday with their daughter, who was working there. On the way, we met up with Jeremy and Ramy, his wife, at the Buffalo Yacht Club happily learning she was pregnant, and again with Jeremy in New York. Erica and Leo, her husband-to-be, came for a week with us in Lucaya. Our week together with friends and family exploring the local coastline and Lucaya was a welcome rest from our daily travelling to the Bahamas. One night, we had a 13-people dinner party on our boat, which was a great get-together with many jokes and much laughter.

We had enjoyed crossing the States and the many daily challenges but by the time we had explored the Exumas, George Town, Eluthera and Abacos in the Bahamas, we decided that this transient life was not quite what it had been when we were younger, travelling with our two children. Perhaps it was because we did not have the long-distance, 20-day offshore trips, which provided a consistent daily life with just a 360-degree horizon when we were on our own with no possible daily help. I am not sure about the real reason. In addition, though, Jeremy and Ramy now had a baby called Riley that we wanted to enjoy for a few weeks before heading to England to meet up with Erica and Leo, her fiancé, who were going to get married in June 1998.

So after we left the Bahamas with the experience of meeting the friendly people, going aground many times, going aground out of sight of land, a disturbing first for us, pulling boats off reefs, enjoying the warm waters and superb yellow beaches, many isolated, and experiencing 60 mph winds at night anchorages, we headed back to Florida. There we had the boat sold, making $3–4,000 on it, and headed up to Toronto to be with Jeremy, Ramy and Riley. I later wrote *French Silk on Water* about this trip.

During our time in the Bahamas, and afterwards, we were often in contact with three particular boats: Dennis and Sue on *Sandpiper*, Dave and Beverley on *Cloverleaf* and Marty and Ellen on *Dragonfly*.

In 1999 an email arrived from Marty, whom we had helped in the Bahamas, asking us if we would like to join him and his friend in Georgetown, Bahamas to help bring *Dragonfly* back to Charleston. We thought this a great "do it now" opportunity for some more sailing and immediately said, "Yes." When getting our flight out of Miami for Georgetown, we actually found we were on the same plane as they were. It was a delightful three-week trip which had three special moments.

Once, while anchored, a dingy passed, and we saw its name, *Cloverleaf*. We had met Dave and Beverley in their sailboat called *Cloverleaf* in a hurricane refuge while on our earlier Bahamas trip when bad weather was forecasted. Calling out, we were told that

Dave and Beverley were in the next bay in a 61 ft Krogan power boat, having sold their sailboat. That was a wonderful surprise meeting. We dinghied round to see them again and it led to an invitation from them five years later to join them in Turkey for a tour in *Cloverleaf* which is described in Chapter 26.

A few days later in another bay, we amazingly encountered *Sandpiper* with Denis and Sue who had stayed on cruising for another year. How lucky can you get? We had an enjoyable catch-up supper on their catamaran that night and rowed back in the calm sea with the moon creating shadows of fish on the sand bottom.

The third surprise occurred when passing Cape Canaveral at night on the way back to Charleston, as a satellite was launched and roared overhead thundering its way into space. That was an incredible thrill, and I just managed to get Heather out of her bunk in time to see it.

After Erica and Leo's wedding on 13 June 1998, when back in Vancouver re-connecting with all our friends, we looked for another boat. Since selling *Sky One Hundred,* we had bought and sold five sailing boats of different types. We were always looking for something better, depending on the cash available, of course.

CHAPTER 24

Trekking in Nepal
2002

I had just finished a game of tennis at our club when up strolled our friend, Frits Tenge, for the next game. I said, "Frits, I haven't seen you for a while, what have you been up to?" He told me he and wife, Jan, had been trekking in Nepal up to the Annapurna base camp and if we were interested, we could come over and see their pictures. The pictures and tales were inspiring, and I started visualizing this trip for us. We came home planning the trek we wanted to do. Within six weeks, being the right season, we were on a plane to Kathmandu.

We had considered joining a tour group expedition but thought at our ages, 70 and 66, we might not be able to match their pace and in any case, they were expensive. Their route, The Circuit, was the normal tour trek, anticlockwise with a climb over the Thorung La Pass (17,700 ft). We declined the latter trek as possibly too arduous and a likely problem with altitude. I had had a fairly severe altitude problem before in Bolivia on a mining project.

In the Nepal newspaper, I saw an advertisement by a Nepalese guide, Chayngba. We emailed him telling him this is the route we want to do: head up to Annapurna base camp (13,600 ft), head up towards the Thorung La Pass and Muktinath (12,250 ft) but not over it, head down and then cross into the deepest gorge in the world along the Kali Gandaki River towards Mustang, Nepal. The route is between the 8,000-metre peaks of Annapurna (26,700 ft) and Dhawalagiri (26,830 ft), 2,200 ft lower than Everest. I also wanted to make a side trip up to the Dhawalagiri icefall at about 12,600 ft. He replied, "Dear Sir Patrick..." so he got the job!

Chayngba and his small flip-flopped porter, Gancha, were

really good and looked after us as we trekked together for three weeks. The vistas of these huge mountains stirred our spirits. The tea houses along the route, where we stayed, cost about four Mars bars a night. We used to play pick-a-stick using matches against the guides, porters and tourists, or even "spoons." There was always something to do at the end of a long day's hike. The trekkers' drink seemed to be hot lemon tea, which we would be given at 6 a.m. when we started a two-hour trek before stopping for breakfast. After getting to the Annapurna base camp, I had a slight touch of altitude sickness in spite of my Diamox pill (for altitude), but Heather did not. A quote from my diary at Annapurna base camp read: *"During the night, I had to get up for nature's call as a result of my pill. Outside, there was a nearly full moon, a cloudless sky, no wind, and super clear stars everywhere. I stood there in my long johns soaking up this very magical moment. The ring of mountains was brilliantly lit and almost threatening in their stillness. There was no sound. Suddenly I was cold and returned to my warm bunk."*

Next day, we hiked down and crossed into the Kali Gandaki valley, the deepest in the world being between 8,000-feet peaks. From Larjung (8,850 ft) I left early, with Chayngba and Gancha, hiking up to near the icefall in six hours. Heather had a day off. There were no roads; we heard no motors in any of our trekking. There were just tracks and steps. On some trails there were so many steps I wondered if my legs would work the next day. After a while though, on this trek, the trail faded out, and we made our way up a steep, rough tufted grass slope. My companions kept a careful eye on me to see I did not fall. The huge view from the top around 12,500 ft was fantastic as we looked across the valley towards the Annapurna mountains streaming away into the distance.

On the way back, their watch was so close down this steep slope that Gancha's hand was touching me many times to make sure I did not fall. At one time I stopped them and made them laugh when I asked Chayngba if Gancha was falling in love with me because he kept holding my hand. When we got on the flat, I stopped them again and got another laugh when I asked if Gancha was not in love with me anymore because he had stopped holding my hand.

Further up the valley, we reached the very old town of Kagbeni, Nepal at 9,217 ft. It is a village in the Upper Mustang of the Himalayas. To enter Mustang would cost us $700 US each, so we declined.

The land was quite dry and barren now with splashes of green where fields had been irrigated. Huge rolling slopes seemed close to their natural angle of repose. Caravans of mules going north and south passed close by or way off on the alluvial flats looking like some kind of centipedes. Heather and I had looked amongst the thousands of rocks along the trail for dark black stones which, when cracked open, might reveal a sea anemone which are said to be 130 million years old.

Our room here had an excellent view of Mt. Tilicho, 23,160 ft. The town has an old fort and is medieval. It is a warren of narrow alleyways, turns and tunnels. Above, many prayer flags were brilliantly lit in the raking sunrays. Low dark doorways, many dilapidated, looked as if they might collapse outwards at any moment. Wonderfully carved old wood windows embellished many walls. In one quite quiet alleyway, two horses gently nuzzled each other to the tinkle of their neck bells. The whole impression was of a past age. Was this a film set? Would Humphrey Bogart and Lauren Bacall emerge from the shadows?

We were fortunate we had not had four to six hours hiking up a continuous series of steps to reach this point. This kind of experience previously had caused a problem with a two feet squat toilet. The innovation from the Continent caused some major strategic problems because after a long climb, we found our knees partially seized up. Although squatting was maybe just possible, trying to stand up again was not a simple reality and required some innovation as there was nothing to hang onto. Fortunately, our tea house this time had a western toilet.

At the end of the trip, Heather and I took a flight to get a close-up picture of Mt Everest. On another day, we made a one-day hike in the back country to see a very old temple and life in the country. On the way, a religious couple insisted on painting a red religious bindi mark on our foreheads.

It was a fantastic vacation, and we encouraged Jeremy to take it, which he did later with Michael, my brother Michael's son and his wife, Val.

CHAPTER 25

GBS, Paralyzed for a Month
2003 onwards

After our wonderful trek in Nepal, we were thinking about seeing some more of Europe and wondering about the best way to do this. Having read there were so many canals, and especially as we had earlier experienced the Canal de Bourgogne, we thought we might look for a small power boat in England and take it across to France. We planned to use it on the canals there during the summer, put it on land for the winter, and return again for the next summer. Looking at English advertisements, we thought we could buy one for less than $7,000. The idea steadily firmed up so that in February 2003, we flew to England to find a boat.

We had a stopover in Iceland when I found I was not feeling up to scratch and had a sore throat. In England we stayed with Erica and family and started calling people who were selling their boats. Strangely, some would say, "It is all wrapped up for the winter, do you seriously want to see it?" My response was, "Do you want to sell it, because we have come from Canada looking to buy a boat, maybe yours." After two weeks of visiting marinas and river-side berths, we finally bought a 22-foot petrol-fired power boat. During this time, which was a very wearing process, often on rotten days, Roger, Heather's brother, decided he liked the idea, and we were pleased he came in for a half share. We had it put on the hard the Friday before we left for Vancouver and said we would be back in two months.

Next day, when I went to get out of bed, I had a worrying shock. I found my legs folded up and would not support me. I got back into bed, telling Heather, "I have to think about what is happening to me." A week earlier, I had experienced tingling in my fingertips, and later learnt this was the first sign of GBS

(Guillain-Barre Syndrome). After breakfast, I went with Heather to a local doctor, who, after administering various tests, said I had had a TIA (a mild stroke). Later that day, when working on a computer I started missing keys and had Heather and Erica take me to emergency at a hospital near Farnham, Surrey, as I was now quite concerned about these unknowns that were happening to me.

After many more tests, I was told I had some nerve problem (Erica had thought earlier that was my problem after checking on the internet) and I should stay in the hospital for the night. After two days, following a lumbar puncture, they advised I had GBS.

In simple terms, GBS is when your immune system, for some reason, attacks the peripheral nervous system (nerves that radiate from the spinal cord), firstly attacking the myelin protection around the nerve (the axon) and then the axon. The extent of the attack will determine the amount of damage done, and whether the nervous system will fully or only partially recover, leaving you with possible permanent damage. In the worst case, some 18% of people will die. Others will suffer from some permanent level of muscular problems. GBS only attacks one or two people in 100,000. These were not good facts to know about, in spite of many reassurances by the staff that I would get better.

With the confirmation of GBS, treatment followed with a series of intravenous immunoglobulin injections of an immune system from a fit person. After the first night in hospital, I could not hold a book up to read any more and was paralyzed for some 26 days during which I could not move my legs or much of my body. At the same time, I was in considerable pain, only relieved by having my legs regularly moved by others to different positions. This was a huge task for Heather, who often hired a nurse to help overnight. My ability to breathe declined, and I was close to needing a respiratory system to help me breathe until I started to recover. It was a desperately worrying situation, and Jeremy came over from Vancouver to help Heather. After three weeks, I was getting more positive about recovery, especially when finally, with help, I could stand again for all of two minutes.

I was then moved to a rehabilitation hospital where physios and others set about trying to get my body back into shape again. On arrival, physios asked, "Can you walk?" and when I said, "No," two physios, while holding me on either side, took me down a corridor shouting, "Walk! walk!" As I tried, my legs flew out in all directions. When we turned around at the end and I sat in a wheelchair, I was so overcome with emotion that I cried, believing that I might walk again. When they said, "Do you want to try again?" I said, "Yes."

Each morning I would get up before breakfast and exercise up and down in the corridor in my wheelchair. Sometimes I would get up and reach for the end bed frame where, hanging on, I'd do a series of knee bends. I was determined to get myself in normal shape again.

Thirty days later I could walk four hundred yards, and I left to return to Vancouver when I was now probably more than 90% recovered. At home, I began a series of walking exercises starting with just walking around the top of our driveway, then increasing to up and down our driveway and finally to up and down the hill we lived on. Sometimes I knew I had overdone it when muscles seemed to stiffen up and I had to slow down or almost stop. Later I started short sprints on the lawn to make the body move faster. My big mental improvement was walking back onto the tennis courts and having half-hour hits with the coach. From then on, things got better.

From the moment I had entered the hospital and rehab centre in Surrey, England, everyone kept saying, "You are going to get better," a super positive process when you do not know what the problem is, and do not think you are recovering. I have visited some people who had GBS, and always suggested they keep a daily diary of movement so they can appreciate the smallest gain in improvement, and realize they are making progress.

I should mention that another nuisance was the bedpan, which felt like some relic from the days of the Inquisition, but our BC insurance was more of a problem. When we returned, our company said that they were only paying half the cost as we had misinterpreted the agreement terms. We argued to no avail. So Heather and I called up five of their branch offices, said we were thinking of joining, and asked how they interpreted this clause. They agreed with us, and when we let their head office know this, they wrote back saying that "in fairness," they would pay. Once we had banked the check, after all this trouble, we wrote back saying it was not a case of fairness. We had identified a loophole which would save them money in the future and in return, we would like a 50% discount on our next year's fee. Strangely, we did not get a reply.

I am co-author of the book on Guillain-Barre Syndrome *Five Years Later* published by Trafford.

CHAPTER 26

More Adventures
2004–6

In 2004 we received an email from Dave and Bev Defeiges, whom we had met in the Bahamas. They told us they'd had *Cloverleaf* shipped over to the Mediterranean and had cruised to Marmaris, Turkey. Surprisingly, they kindly asked us to join them cruising for three weeks, if I felt recovered enough from GBS. Having already flotilla sailed in that area, which was wonderful, with our "do it now" outlook, we replied we would.

When we arrived, we were provided with our own cabin and bathroom in this very large boat. Dave was happy with the large bottle of gin we gave them as gin and tonic was his favourite drink, and ours. They were a charming couple and we felt very welcome. In their relationship, Bev did all the steering and navigation while Dave ran the engines and mechanical works. I did not like to think what it cost to fill the diesel tanks. In the afternoon I might have a sleep to help my recovery and in the evenings after a long happy hour, we played cards and games and decided where to go the next day.

We toured for three weeks in southeast Turkey looking at many old Roman edifices and hired a car to see some interior ruins. Being early May, there were not many tourists around, and the chance of being able to tour the sites with few people there was a pleasant opportunity.

We often just dinghied ashore and walked through the ruins. Seeing so many, I could not but admire the influence and development by the Romans of their planning, designing and building of these marvellous structures. Their arenas were masterpieces and although usually carved out of a hillside, an impressive one was built on flat ground, so soil had to be brought in to build up supports for all the tunnels and the seating. Bridges sometimes did not last as Romans did not seem to understand the force of water currents which attacked the foundations. The carvings of all structures were always impressive. My question was, how did they get the local populace to build these edifices? Did they bring in teams of experts to show them the way to do the work? Did they pay them? Or were they slaves?

Bev and Dave asked us to stay on for what would have been an intriguing three-week flotilla tour around the eastern Mediterranean but, unfortunately, we had to decline as we had our power boat in England and planned to take it on the French canals. We said warm goodbyes and bussed up to the famous Ephesus site built in the 10th century BC — magnificent — before flying out from Istanbul. Back in England, we decided with Roger that we would sell our boat.

In 2006, Heather was excited she had been invited to play tennis in Manavgat, Turkey in October, for Canada, in the 70s group. I decided to go as coach and ball boy for this ten-day event. Heather played some excellent singles and doubles matches but was at some disadvantage as all matches were on gravel courts versus the hard courts we normally play on. I did take the liberty of suggesting to the team captain that she should encourage the team to be more supportive even when a member was losing. I think cheering and clapping always helped.

Towards the end of the tournament, I hired a car and planned that we would drive to Cappadocia and Pamukkale, both extraordinary tourist areas. In fact, we found our trip was fascinating and the people friendly. We were often invited into a home for a coffee or apple tea where there were many smiles due to the lack of English. In Istanbul, the Blue Mosque was totally staggering in size and structure. One column was at least twenty feet in diameter, and the roof was way up above our heads.

We stopped at Pamukkale first, a 350 km drive, and stayed in a small pension-type hotel. Next day, in this World Heritage site we saw some Roman ruins, but our key interest was to walk on the calcium-covered terraces which were absolutely white due to calcium waters that flowed from hot springs above. We had to remove our shoes to prevent its wear but it made our feet sore, so we ended up with a swim in the hot springs, as had the Romans.

For two days we drove some 650 km to Cappadocia in the centre of Turkey, southeast of Ankara, its capital. It is a vast area of soft sandstone where people in the past and present have dug out caves and passages and lived as deep as 100 metres underground. It is said Christians retreated underground when enemies came.

We drove into the small town of Goreme and stopped a couple of nights at the Blue Moon Hotel, simply because it was the name of our power boat. Next morning, we found a layer of snow had fallen and so we explored an underground cave system. It had several floor levels with steep, narrow stairs connecting each floor. "Narrow" meant my elbows often touched the walls and the ceiling was so low that I had to bend forward going down in order not to touch the ceiling. A big problem was waiting for a break in those coming up so that we could go down. Although there were many rooms, kitchens and even a church below, it was not good for claustrophobics. The whole concept of living underground meant the lighting required was formidable. I was impressed but glad when we left there; although I like caves, I am not a troglodyte.

Next day was sunny and calm with a number of colourful hot air balloons overhead. We did not try one but researched the vast number of natural sandstone shapes, some carved, some weather-beaten, all perforated with window and door openings leading to carved-out areas inside. The landscape was an amazing sight because of all the different rock shapes and sizes which could be seen in all directions. Heather and I were happy we had come on this long drive to experience such a unique piece of history.

CHAPTER 27

Where to Now?
2007 onwards

Back in Vancouver, Heather and I began to feel the urge to make a trip to Nepal again, as we'd had such an enjoyable time before. I ask myself how these urges arise but I am not sure why, except the push to do something different. Perhaps travel and seeing new scenes is the attraction. Even as I write this, I think ahead to where I might be travelling up some back road in an isolated area. This time we thought we would make a trip to the Everest base camp at 17,500 ft. It was an optimistic plan, as we were gaining in years, but our previous guide, Chayngba, was willing to take us.

Four weeks before leaving (near Christmas), Heather got a dose of pneumonia and was advised not to make the trip. It was a big disappointment for both of us. Since it was all organized, I decided to go, and Chayngba met me, with hugs, at the airport as usual. He had flights organized, and two days later we were flown up to Lukla at 9,200 ft. Because of the cloudiness in this region, we had to pause temporarily at a lower-level emergency area, landing uphill on a very steep gravelly slope. We waited there for two hours before being able to head for our destination when we took off downhill to land uphill at Lukla. There we hiked downwards for a night at Phakding at 8,700 ft.

Frits Tenge, our tennis friend, had advised that I should stay here for two nights to acclimatize properly. Feeling okay, I did not do this, but next day we made a seven-hour continuous uphill climb and into the lowest part of Namche Bazaar, 11,350 ft. NB was the point from which most trekkers organize for the climb to the base camp. I was completely knackered, having climbed too high too fast. I realized that I still had GBS problems and my stamina level was a lot lower. There were many times when I

233

stopped to get my wind back while younger bodies passed me. After two days of rest, I was still lacking in energy and advised my guide I was not going to continue further as I did not wish to be a liability. This was a big disappointment to me and a lesson in the altitude rules. In any case, I was 75. I have just re-read Heather's letter to me in Nepal in which the Tenges had told her, "Flying into that altitude, with the short climb down followed by the big climb up to NB was the toughest climb they had done." On my return, I joined Heather in England and we had a relaxed holiday with our families.

While Heather and I continue our tennis, golf, cruising, bridge and occasional hikes, we have to admit aches and pains are increasing so that fixed holidays, such as two weeks in our favourite Mexican vacation spot (just around Christmas) at Las Brisas, Huatulco, an ex-Club Med facility, are always welcome for a complete rest. It is a pleasant, friendly resort for tennis, sailing, swimming and snorkeling, with three beaches. Much of my time since 2011 has been spent writing books about my travels, giving talks and selling my books, while time seems to slip by. "Is it actually getting faster?" Sometimes I wonder, especially since it is some 15 years since I had GBS.

We are blessed with a great set of friends, most of whom we've known for years and who are incredibly supportive, and many we have been with on vacations. When we returned from my two-month GBS problem in England, I thought our garden would be completely overgrown. Imagine our surprise as we drove up the steep driveway and saw lawns cut and everything in perfect order. Friends, I am sure, had worked their butts off to do that for us as had others, who had looked after Chris, Heather's dad, at times while we were cruising in the Bahamas. And there are many others, too numerous to name who have helped. We are really fortunate to have such a super and close-knit group of friends.

With so many cruise ships touring the world, we have drifted into this way of seeing different sights. Cruises can be expensive, however. Most shipping companies are out to remove your money, and we have found the best savings can be made by booking trips at the last possible minute, while arranging our own side trips rather than taking the ones provided by cruise lines. It is also best to book your own plane flight to pick up a ship.

On our first cruise, we had pre-booked a seven-day cruise to Glacier Bay and back from Vancouver. At breakfast on the morning we had to make the final payment, I saw an advertisement for a 14-day trip, going to Glacier Bay and onto Prince William Sound returning the same way. As it was only 20% more, I immediately booked this 14-day cruise and cancelled the seven-day one. Heather was extra happy as there was no cooking for two weeks. This trip gave us the opportunity of seeing some bays twice, an advantage, as it is less likely to be fogged in on both visits.

On another occasion, in 2015, we thought it was time to bring the whole family together before the children went their separate ways. None had been on a cruise ship, so we booked a seven-day cruise to Glacier Bay for nine of us, Heather's brother Roger, our son, Jeremy and his daughter Riley, and our daughter, Erica, her husband Leo and their daughters Ellen and Kira. It was chaos in our condo for a few nights, but once on the ship, we rarely saw the children until supper, when the Indonesian crew treated us royally with their jokes and puzzles. The three girls slept unofficially in one cabin. Heather went in there once but never again, as it was in such a mess.

We later decided to go on a cruise to St. Petersburg from Copenhagen. Knowing that Jens and Anni Bang, who used to work with me, lived nearby and might be there from their main home in Nairobi, we sent an email to tell them of our arrival in Denmark. By another one of those amazing coincidences, it turned out that they were at home and Anni was returning to Nairobi the afternoon of the day we arrived back from our cruise to fly back to the UK. So we were able to meet, enjoy a few beers and lunch, and were driven around in the local park in our own horse-driven carriage which they had arranged. Jens took us back to the airport, and after many warm hugs, we went our separate ways.

At St. Petersburg, our most delightful stop, we saw spectacular displays of richness from the past in the Hermitage Museum. I particularly enjoyed the tour because while concentrating on a painting, I got separated from my tour group. This was a treat, as I was able to wander around on my own and take my time absorbing the wealth people had once lived with. I thought that as a reminder of Leningrad under siege (over two years and the longest ever), when the Germans tried to starve them out, authorities might have left one block of destroyed buildings to be seen by tourists, as an example of how the population had suffered.

Another year, we flew to Miami and took a 10-day cruise to the beginning of the Panama Canal and back — a reminder that my father had been there during its construction. Cartagena's massive hilltop fort built in the 1600s was most impressive. I had a chat with a guide and learned the Spanish brought the gold they had obtained inland, down the River Magdalena to Barranquilla at its mouth, and from there they shipped it to Spain. Sir Francis Drake used to wait there to capture them. To avoid this piracy the Spanish cut the Canal del Dique higher up the river and out to the sea.

After this cruise, I suggested to Heather that at our age, either one of us might have a health problem that would make travelling difficult, so perhaps we should do another cruise. Six weeks later, we flew to Lima in Peru and boarded a cruise vessel stopping at various places down the coast, including Valparaiso, Puerto Montt and into the sheltered islands of southern Chile. Here we cruised close to various tidewater glaciers which were not as stirring as those in Alaska. Cruising past the north side of Cape Horn on our way was impressive though, as a nearly 60-knot wind was churning the sea into a white mass. I wondered what would happen if we ever had engine failure. Further on, the weather was too bad to allow the ship to dock at the Falkland Islands so we pushed on to Buenos Aires. This cruise line, Oceania, which advertised two for the price of one, had, to my mind, excessive charges for their shore trips. After two trips, we were getting bored with the daily routine and decided we'd had enough cruising for a while.

So where to now? It is difficult to look into the future without the benefits of a fit young body because active opportunities are less feasible. I think the time is getting close to making a last trip in our small power boat in Vancouver and then selling it. Heather argues that it is expensive to keep and is only used one month a year. She is right but to leave behind such a warm fraternity we have been associated with over the years will be a loss. Just earlier this year as we docked, we knew three people there, one that recognized us by name, where we had met 39 years ago. The others were a doctor friend, Paul and his wife, Doreen. Paul had equipped us with a medical kit when we left in *Sky One Hundred* for our South Seas trip. I remember him telling us how to give an injection without hitting the sciatic nerve. Meetings with sailing friends would be missed.

We like to be as active as possible, and we still have the whole of BC to see, so perhaps we should go exploring in a camper taking our golf clubs and tennis rackets with us. We are fortunate at 86 and 81 to be fit enough to do this. If I am up at the Whistler ski resort with Norman and Gloria or Jamie and Patsy, our good friends, and I look up and see skiers speeding down the slopes, I get a surge of memories and past delights from skiing downhill with all the twists and turns. Perhaps I had better get fitter, which Jeremy keeps urging me to do, as he does with his partner, Jenni. Maybe I should get more into bridge to keep the mind going or perhaps I have enough energy and interest to write a couple more books.

I have several times mentioned that Heather has been a positive supporter of any plans we put together in search of adventure. Each time I have said how lucky I am that we are together. What I have not mentioned is the number of times strangers have approached Heather over the years, sometimes when I was with her, complimenting her on her beauty and wanting to give her a hug. It just happened again on our recent holiday to Las Brisas, Mexico, when a lady approached her saying,

"You are so lovely" and gave her a hug. It was her second surprise in Mexico, as her brother, Roger and his new friend, Carol had arrived the day before from England as a surprise, knowing we would be there.

The nearest thing I've experienced to a compliment occurred recently when waiting for an MRI in a hospital, after telling the nurse my name and age. Suddenly, a voice beside me said, "What's your secret?" I turned and saw an elderly lady sitting there, and said, "What do you mean, what's my secret?" She replied, "You have no wrinkles, and you are fifteen years older than me," so I said, "You look okay to me, but I have been with my super wife for sixty years."

Now our key delights are seeing how our children and their children are progressing and where their adventures take them.

Best wishes to all

APPENDIX

1934–1945

Summarised below is a list of key events showing how Hitler rose to power and started World War II. My comments are in *italics*.

1934

July: As a member of the Nazi party, Hitler became the Führer of Germany.

1935

March: Hitler introduced military conscription and announced the formation of the German air force.

June: A bi-lateral Anglo-German Naval Agreement allowed Germany to increase its navy to one-third the size of Britain's navy. (*France disagreed with this English appeasement policy.*)

1936

March: Germany re-militarized the Rhineland by the French border.

October: Germany formed an alliance with Italy.

1937

November: Germany made a military agreement with Japan.

1938

March: Germany annexed Austria.

September 30: In the Munich Agreement, Britain and France allowed Germany to annex the German-speaking part of Czechoslovakia (*An unbelievable step in Prime Minister Chamberlain's appeasement policy, along with that of France, with the intention of preventing another war. Czechoslovakia was not present.*)

During this five-year period, Britain and France tried to maintain a level of appeasement with Hitler in the belief that Germany would maintain peace and a war would not be required to keep Hitler under control. Chamberlain, prime minister of England, who had led the appeasement policy, convinced the British public he had established a compromise in the Munich

Agreement that conflict with Hitler would be avoided. Regretfully, just six months later we were at war when Hitler occupied the whole of Czechoslovakia and invaded Poland. Britain and France were forced to declare war against Germany to support their treaty obligations.

1939

March: Germany annexed the remainder of Czechoslovakia.

March: Britain and France pledged aid to Poland if attacked.

May: US Senate blocked aid to Britain and France in case of war.

August: Germany made a non-aggression pact with Russia.

September 1: Germany attacked Poland from the west; Russia attacked from the east on September 17.

September 3: Britain, Australia, New Zealand and France declared war against Germany. It was the second war with Germany in 21 years.

September 5: United States declared neutrality except for sale of materials and arms.

Churchill had no doubts about Hitler's long-term territorial objectives, but he was not able to convince members of parliament of the danger of Hitler's continued expansion and development of German military resources. I wonder what the members of parliament were thinking about, not to believe Churchill's warnings. Surely in the last four years there had been enough evidence of the danger? However, their senses returned only after Britain declared war, and Churchill was made First Lord of the Admiralty, and seven months later was elected prime minister of a coalition of parties to run the country.

Life passed along pleasantly in these early days, with little sign of the actual war. It was a period called the Phony War, because there was no sign of the Germans or their planes. It continued to about April 1940.

1940

April 9: Nazis invaded Denmark and Norway.

May 10: Holland surrendered to the Nazis (*in just five days*).

May 26: Britain evacuated 400,000 troops from Dunkirk

(needed to defend the UK).

June 10: Norway surrendered to Germany.

June 22: France lay down its arms and signed an armistice with Germany. *(This, just eight months after Germany's invasion of Poland, the start of war.)*

July 1: The Battle of Britain started (*England's air defence against the Luftwaffe*).

The pace at which Germany invaded and caused countries to surrender was a new technique based on speed and surprise, known as "Blitzkrieg." It worked so well that British and French forces, fighting against their Nazi invaders in northern France, were caught unaware and separated. The mainly British forces had to retreat to Dunkirk where an Armada of some 800 British naval ships, fishing boats and private recreational boats crossed the Channel many times in a week to rescue the troops – an absolute requirement to bring back our troops for the defence of England. During this time, they were being attacked and bombed by the Luftwaffe. Churchill called the rescue "a miracle of deliverance," but he said the events in France "were a colossal disaster." There were thoughts by some in England of seeking an unconditional surrender with Germany, but not Churchill, who out-maneuvered them. Hitler decided the German military needed to regroup and consolidate its advance rather than continuing to attack with the intent of invading England. It was fortunate, as England was in a weak position militarily.

With the surrender of France, Britain, with its Commonwealth countries, was essentially on its own against the might of Germany. Roosevelt in the United States took a position of neutrality, essentially to maintain his presidential position as many Americans were not ready to support Britain.

The French armistice with Germany, signed by Marshal Pétain, gave Germany full control and occupation of the French north coast (to attack England) and the west coast (for the Battle of the Atlantic). The rest of France, called Vichy France, was given magnanimously by Hitler to function under the general control of Marshal Pétain along with control of the French fleet from 1940–

241

44 in what might be called a collaborationist government. Acting for the Germans, they rounded up Jews and communists to be sent to concentration camps, fought against French resistance groups, and against Britain and its Allies. At that time, there was a firm belief that England could not win the war against Germany and that it would surrender or be taken within the next six to eight weeks. In fact, Hitler apparently sent a note to the English suggesting they join Germany under his rule.

Churchill's actions were contrary to any form of appeasement or surrender, so it is surprising that most members of Parliament followed

Chamberlain's appeasement policy. After war was declared against Germany, Churchill was concerned about the French fleet in Mer-el-Kebir, French Algeria, being taken over by the Germans. He sent a naval task force with instructions to ask the Vichy commander there to leave and join the English fleet. The French commander contacted Admiral Darlan, commander of the French navy, who amazingly declined this request; had he not grasped the power of Hitler and his intentions? He perhaps thought this would not be viewed favourably by the Germans if England were to surrender. So, following a final one-hour warning by the English to join them or be shelled, they were shelled, and much of the French fleet was sunk in the harbour. This and similar actions to control the French fleet (including boarding French ships that had already moved to England) made the world, including the United States, realize the power and determination of the English to fight the evil of Hitler. Joe Kennedy, the American ambassador in 1940, who kept telling Roosevelt that Britain was going to surrender or lose the war, was sent back to America by Churchill.

Strangely, in 1941, when Vichy French forces, controlled Syria and Lebanon, they fought against English and Allied forces. Again, in 1942, when the Germans needed to occupy Vichy France, the French scuttled 77 of their remaining warships in Toulon. Most did not try to sail to join English naval forces. *Prenez garde*, we had been supporting the French who had been our Allies.

With Hitler still intent on invading England, he needed to eliminate the air force, which would attack his invading forces. Through the summer and autumn of 1940, the Luftwaffe maintained a continuous attack of British airfields, radar stations, the RAF, and production factories. In what was called the Battle of Britain, Hurricanes and Spitfires fought off bombers supported by Messerschmitts as they attacked in waves. After three or four months, Germany realized it was not winning this crucial battle, which was considered their first major defeat. Germany had lost some 2,000 aircraft to Britain's 1,000. Most of the British and Allied pilots were young and many recently trained. Churchill's famous praise for them was "never in the field of human conflict was so much owed by so many to so few."

On September 7, 1940, Hitler changed his direction of attack, and started a bombing Blitz, mainly of London and the docks, but also of other major cities in England. This continued until May 1941. The first raid on London came late one afternoon when over 600 bombers and 1,000 fighters dropped bombs over a two-hour period, causing absolute chaos. When they departed, the next wave came in, dropping bombs for a further two hours assisted by the light of all the fires below. On any day you could see some ten planes but imagine seeing the number of Luftwaffe planes sent with death and destruction in mind. Hearing the drone of the planes, the heavy thumping of the ack-ack guns, the whistle of falling bombs, the roaring crash of their explosions and those from landmines on parachutes caused fear. But the surrounding fires, caused by "breadbaskets," which were canisters filled with a hundred incendiary bombs, were highly destructive. Buildings collapsed and fires were everywhere. Firemen and police tried to maintain control and volunteers helped to get people out of ruined buildings and into ambulances. Searchlights wove across the darkness, searching for enemy planes. The next morning, services still ran, and people picked their way through rubble to get to work. During these raids, the Germans were steadily increasing the size of their bombs.

The bombing lasted six months in an attempt to reduce the

populace to its knees and instigate surrender. Not so, as it had the opposite effect in further uniting the spirit of the people against Germany. Around May 1941, a "V for victory" hand sign was started and was frequently seen. At the same time the "dot, dot, dot, dash" Morse signal for V began on the radio. These signals were to encourage the population and tell occupied peoples that we were winning, and encourage a positive outlook about the war.

During my school years, the war continued with these key events.

1940

July: The Vichy French broke off relations with Britain when the British Navy destroyed the French fleet at Mer-el-Kebir in French Africa. (*What were the Vichy French going to do with the fleet?*)[1] Amazingly, as a result, the Vichy wanted to declare war against the British.

September: Italy invaded Egypt and Britain started an offensive against Italy.

1941

April: Yugoslavia and Greece surrendered to Germany.

June: Germany attacked Russia (*a complete reversal of their earlier pact*).

August: Nazis started the siege of Leningrad (St. Petersburg).

December 5: Germany abandoned its attack on Moscow.

December 7: Japan attacked the US Fleet at Pearl Harbour. (*Churchill now believes US will enter the war.*)

December 8: US and Britain declared war on Japan.

December 11: Hitler declared war on the US.

December 11: US declared war on Germany. (*Churchill was much relieved.*)

1942

May 3: 1,000 RAF bombers attacked Cologne.

November: Operation Torch in North Africa, first US military action against Germany and Vichy France.

---

[1] Smith, Colin, 2009. *England's Last War Against France: Fighting Vichy 1940-1942*. Weidenfeld & Nicolson: Great Britain.

1944

September: Montgomery drove back German General Rommel's forces in Egypt.

June 6: D-Day, British, America, Canadian forces and others landed in Normandy, France. *(In the military, D-Day is the day on which a combat attack or operation is to be initiated.)*

July 28: Russia drove the Germans back to their original borders.

1945

May 8: VE Day *(Victory in Europe)* as Germany surrendered.

June 21: Battle of Okinawa ended.

August: The US dropped an atom bomb on Hiroshima and one on Nagasaki on August 9, killing 150,000.

August 8: Russia declared war on Japan.

August 14: VJ Day *(Victory in Japan)* as Japan surrendered.

In the final stages of the war, Hitler, in his desperate attempts to demoralize Londoners, sent over V1 rockets, known as doodlebugs or buzz bombs. These auto-piloted machines with a jet engine located over the back end of the fuselage and the nose packed with explosives, would fall on timed engine stoppage. When one stopped, it would glide on, dive to the ground and explode.

Beginning in June 1944, over 10,000 rockets were fired at southeast England, 2,500 of which were aimed mainly at London. Sometimes 100 a day would be fired. As well as trying to shoot them down from the ground, fighter planes were stripped down so they could exceed 400 miles per hour and shoot them down or tip up one wing, so they dived into the ground. Ack-ack guns and captive balloons might also bring them down. They finally stopped in March 1945.

In the last stages of the war, Hitler sent over much larger V2 rockets, which could not be heard or seen, and which landed with devastating effect and no warning.

On VE Day, or Victory in Europe Day, there was exhilaration and rare gaiety in the air as people relaxed and generally went mad. Street parties were held all over Britain, and any passing military person was treated with considerable passion.

This massive world war lasted six years, the worst war yet. Although estimates vary, some 70 million military and civilians were killed, many more were injured, and many died after the war due to illness, hunger and poor living conditions. It is difficult to understand how a megalomaniac such as Hitler could cause such chaos and destruction in the world. It was such an incredible waste of resources, talent and people, and it was astonishing that he was joined by Russia, Italy and finally Japan all seeking what? More power? More control? Elimination of people they did not like or trust? Churchill certainly breathed a sigh of relief when Pearl Harbour was bombed, and the American people finally joined Britain against our enemies. If the aggressors had won, what would they have done next — fight each other? Would we have won the war if the Americans had not joined in?

One wonders where this fighting ends because there has always been war. Today, there are so many battles throughout the world, small at the moment but liable to explode into something much bigger; it seems nothing creative and positive is derived. Perhaps the final fights will just be about survival over diminishing resources such as water, oil, gas, coal and loss of usable land due to rising sea levels. Imagine the power of a peaceful Germany, if Hitler had used his power to develop creative actions for the benefit of the world.

CPSIA information can be obtained
at www.ICGtesting.com
Printed in the USA
BVHW062010291021
619990BV00001B/1